CROCK·POT
·THE ORIGINAL SLOW COOKER·

BOWLS

Publications International, Ltd.

Louis Weber, CEO
Publications International, Ltd.
8140 Lehigh Ave
Morton Grove, IL 60053

Pictured on the front cover (*clockwise from top*): Hearty Pork and Bacon Chili (*page 54*), Chicken Orzo Soup (*page 108*) and White Chicken Chili (*page 99*).

Pictured on the back cover (*clockwise from top left*): Chunky Ranch Potatoes (*page 129*), Corn Chip Chili (*page 38*), Chickpea and Vegetable Curry (*page 72*), Mixed Berry Cobbler (*page 180*) and Pork Soup with Soba Noodles and Bok Choy (*page 46*).

ISBN: 978-1-68022-768-0

Library of Congress Control Number: 2017931510

Manufactured in China.

8 7 6 5 4 3 2 1

CONTENTS

SLOW COOKING TIPS

SIZES OF CROCK-POT®
SLOW COOKERS

Smaller **CROCK-POT**® slow cookers—such as 1- to 3½-quart models—are the perfect size for cooking for singles, a couple, or empty nesters (and also for serving dips).

While medium-size **CROCK-POT**® slow cookers (those holding somewhere between 3 quarts and 5 quarts) will easily cook enough food at one time to feed a small family. They are also convenient for holiday side dishes or appetizers.

Large **CROCK-POT**® slow cookers are great for large family dinners, holiday entertaining, and potluck suppers. A 6- to 7-quart model is ideal if you like to make meals in advance. Or, have dinner tonight and store leftovers for later.

TYPES OF CROCK-POT®
SLOW COOKERS

Current **CROCK-POT**® slow cookers come equipped with many different features and benefits, from auto cook programs to oven-safe stoneware to timed programming. Please visit **WWW.CROCK-POT.COM** to find the **CROCK-POT**® slow cooker that best suits your needs.

How you plan to use a **CROCK-POT**® slow cooker may affect the model you choose to purchase. For everyday cooking, choose a size large enough to serve your family. If you plan to use the **CROCK-POT**® slow cooker primarily for entertaining, choose one of the larger sizes. Basic **CROCK-POT®** slow cookers can hold as little as 16 ounces or as much as 7 quarts. The smallest sizes are great for keeping dips warm on a buffet, while the larger sizes can more readily fit large quantities of food and larger roasts.

COOKING, STIRRING, AND FOOD SAFETY

CROCK-POT® slow cookers are safe to leave unattended. The outer heating base may get hot as it cooks, but it should not pose a fire hazard. The heating element in the heating base functions at a low wattage and is safe for your countertops.

Your **CROCK-POT®** slow cooker should be filled about one-half to three-fourths full for most recipes unless otherwise instructed. Lean meats such as chicken or pork tenderloin will cook faster than meats with more connective tissue and fat such as beef chuck or pork shoulder. Bone-in meats will take longer than boneless cuts. Typical **CROCK-POT®** slow cooker dishes take approximately 7 to 8 hours to reach the simmer point on LOW and about 3 to 4 hours on HIGH. Once the vegetables and meat start to simmer and braise, their flavors will fully blend and meat will become fall-off-the-bone tender.

According to the U.S. Department of Agriculture, all bacteria are killed at a temperature of 165°F. It's important to follow the recommended cooking times and not to open the lid often, especially early in the cooking process when heat is building up inside the unit. If you need to open the lid to check on your food or are adding additional ingredients, remember to allow additional cooking time if necessary to ensure food is cooked through and tender.

Large **CROCK-POT®** slow cookers, the 6- to 7-quart sizes, may benefit from a quick stir halfway through cook time to help distribute heat and promote even cooking. It's usually unnecessary to stir at all, as even ½ cup liquid will help to distribute heat and the stoneware is the perfect medium for holding food at an even temperature throughout the cooking process.

OVEN-SAFE STONEWARE

All **CROCK-POT®** slow cooker removable stoneware inserts may (without their lids) be used safely in ovens at up to 400°F. In addition, all **CROCK-POT®** slow cookers are microwavable without their lids. If you own another slow cooker brand, please refer to your owner's manual for specific stoneware cooking medium tolerances.

FROZEN FOOD

Frozen food can be successfully cooked in a **CROCK-POT®** slow cooker. However, it will require longer cooking time than the same recipe made with fresh food. Using an instant-read thermometer is recommended to ensure meat is fully cooked.

PASTA AND RICE

If you are converting a recipe for your **CROCK-POT®** slow cooker that calls for uncooked pasta, first cook the pasta on the stovetop just until slightly tender. Then add the pasta to the **CROCK-POT®** slow cooker.

If you are converting a recipe for the **CROCK-POT®** slow cooker that calls for cooked rice, stir in raw rice with the other recipe ingredients plus ¼ cup extra liquid per ¼ cup of raw rice.

BEANS

Beans must be softened completely before combining with sugar and/or acidic foods in the **CROCK-POT®** slow cooker. Sugar and acid have a hardening effect on beans and will prevent softening. Fully cooked canned beans may be used as a substitute for dried beans.

Meatballs and Spaghetti Sauce (page 14)

Chinese Chicken Stew (page 100)

VEGETABLES

Root vegetables often cook more slowly than meat. Cut vegetables accordingly to cook at the same rate as meat—large or small or lean versus marbled—and place near the sides or bottom of the stoneware to facilitate cooking.

HERBS

Fresh herbs add flavor and color when added at the end of the cooking cycle; if added at the beginning, many fresh herbs' flavor will dissipate over long cook times. Ground and/or dried herbs and spices work well in slow cooking and may be added at the beginning of cook time. For dishes with shorter cook times, hearty fresh herbs such as rosemary and thyme hold up well. The flavor power of

all herbs and spices can vary greatly depending on their particular strength and shelf life. Use chili powders and garlic powder sparingly, as these can sometimes intensify over the long cook times. Always taste the finished dish and correct seasonings including salt and pepper.

LIQUIDS

It is not necessary to use more than ½ to 1 cup liquid in most instances. Most juices in meats and vegetables are retained more in slow cooking than in conventional cooking. Excess liquid can be cooked down and concentrated after slow cooking, either on the stovetop or by removing the meat and vegetables from the stoneware. Then stirring in one of the following thickeners and setting the **CROCK-POT®** slow cooker to HIGH. Cover and cook the liquid on HIGH for approximately 15 minutes or until thickened.

FLOUR: All-purpose flour is often used to thicken soups or stews. Stir water into the flour in a small bowl until smooth. With the **CROCK-POT®** slow cooker on HIGH, whisk flour mixture into the liquid in the **CROCK-POT®** slow cooker. Cover; cook on HIGH 15 minutes or until the mixture is thickened.

CORNSTARCH: Cornstarch gives sauces a clear, shiny appearance; it's used most often for sweet dessert sauces and stir-fry sauces. Stir water into the cornstarch in a small bowl until the cornstarch is dissolved. Quickly stir this mixture into the liquid in the **CROCK-POT**® slow cooker; the sauce will thicken as soon as the liquid simmers. Cornstarch breaks down with too much heat, so never add it at the beginning of the slow cooking process and turn off the heat as soon as the sauce thickens.

TAPIOCA: Tapioca is a starchy substance extracted from the root of the cassava plant. Its greatest advantage is that it withstands long cooking, making it an ideal choice for slow cooking. Add tapioca at the beginning of cooking and you'll get a clear, thickened sauce in the finished dish. Dishes using tapioca as a thickener are best cooked on the LOW setting; it may become stringy when boiled for a long time.

MILK

Milk, cream, and sour cream break down during extended cooking. When possible, add them during the last 15 to 30 minutes of slow cooking, until just heated through. Condensed soups may be substituted for milk and may cook for extended times.

FISH

Fish is delicate and should be stirred into the **CROCK-POT**® slow cooker gently during the last 15 to 30 minutes of cooking. Cover; cook just until cooked through and serve immediately.

BAKED GOODS

If you wish to prepare bread, cakes, or pudding cakes in a **CROCK-POT**® slow cooker, you may want to purchase a covered, vented metal cake pan accessory for your **CROCK-POT**® slow cooker. You can also use any straight-sided soufflé dish or deep cake pan that will fit into the stoneware of your unit. Baked goods can be prepared directly in the stoneware; however, they can be a little difficult to remove from the insert, so follow the recipe directions carefully.

Mixed Berry Cobbler (page 180)

HEARTY BEEF & LAMB

Cajun Pot Roast

MAKES 6 SERVINGS

1 boneless beef chuck roast (3 pounds)*

1 to 2 tablespoons Cajun seasoning

1 tablespoon vegetable oil

1 can (about 14 ounces) diced tomatoes

1 can (about 14 ounces) diced tomatoes with mild green chiles

1 medium onion, chopped

1 cup chopped rutabaga

1 cup chopped mushrooms

1 cup chopped turnip

1 cup chopped peeled parsnip

1 cup chopped green bell pepper

1 cup green beans

1 cup sliced carrots

1 cup corn

2 tablespoons hot pepper sauce

1 teaspoon sugar

½ teaspoon black pepper

¾ cup water

*Unless you have a 5-, 6- or 7-quart **CROCK-POT**® slow cooker, cut any roast larger than 2½ pounds in half so it cooks completely.

1 Coat inside of **CROCK-POT**® slow cooker with nonstick cooking spray. Season roast with cajun seasoning. Heat oil in large skillet over medium-high heat. Brown roast 5 minutes on each side.

2 Place roast, tomatoes, onion, rutabaga, mushrooms, turnip, parsnip, bell pepper, green beans, carrots, corn, hot pepper sauce, sugar and black pepper in **CROCK-POT**® slow cooker. Pour in water. Cover; cook on LOW 6 hours.

Mole Chili

MAKES 4 TO 6 SERVINGS

2 corn tortillas, each cut into 4 wedges

1½ pounds boneless beef chuck roast, cut into 1-inch pieces

¾ teaspoon salt, divided

½ teaspoon black pepper, divided

3 tablespoons olive oil, divided

2 medium onions, chopped

5 cloves garlic, minced

1 cup beef broth

1 can (about 14 ounces) fire-roasted diced tomatoes

2 tablespoons chili powder

1 tablespoon ground ancho chili powder

1 teaspoon ground cumin

1 teaspoon dried oregano

¾ teaspoon ground cinnamon

1 can (about 15 ounces) red kidney beans, rinsed and drained

1½ ounces semi-sweet chocolate, chopped

Queso fresco (optional)

Chopped fresh cilantro (optional)

1 Coat inside of **CROCK-POT®** slow cooker with nonstick cooking spray. Place tortillas in food processor or blender; process to fine crumbs. Set aside.

2 Season beef with ½ teaspoon salt and ¼ teaspoon pepper. Heat 1 tablespoon oil in large skillet over medium-high heat. Add half of beef to skillet; cook 4 minutes or until browned. Remove to **CROCK-POT®** slow cooker. Add 1 tablespoon oil to skillet; repeat with remaining beef. Heat remaining 1 tablespoon oil in skillet. Add onions and garlic; cook 2 minutes. Pour broth into skillet, scraping up any browned bits from bottom of skillet. Remove to **CROCK-POT®** slow cooker. Stir in reserved tortilla crumbs, tomatoes, chili powder, ancho chile, cumin, oregano and cinnamon.

3 Cover; cook on LOW 8 to 8½ hours or on HIGH 4 to 4½ hours. Stir in beans. Cover; cook on LOW 30 minutes. Turn off heat. Add chocolate, remaining ¼ teaspoon salt and ¼ teaspoon pepper; stir until chocolate is melted. Top with queso fresco and cilantro, if desired.

Meatballs and Spaghetti Sauce

MAKES 6 TO 8 SERVINGS

2 pounds ground beef

1 cup plain dry bread crumbs

1 onion, chopped

2 eggs, beaten

¼ cup minced fresh Italian parsley

4 teaspoons minced garlic, divided

½ teaspoon dry mustard

½ teaspoon black pepper

4 tablespoons olive oil, divided

1 can (28 ounces) whole tomatoes

½ cup chopped fresh basil

1 teaspoon sugar

Salt and black pepper

Hot cooked spaghetti

1 Combine beef, bread crumbs, onion, eggs, parsley, 2 teaspoons garlic, dry mustard and ½ teaspoon black pepper in large bowl. Form into walnut-sized balls. Heat 2 tablespoons oil in large skillet over medium heat. Brown meatballs on all sides. Remove to **CROCK-POT®** slow cooker.

2 Combine tomatoes, basil, remaining 2 tablespoons oil, remaining 2 teaspoons garlic, sugar, salt and black pepper in medium bowl; stir to blend. Pour over meatballs, turn to coat. Cover; cook on LOW 3 to 5 hours or on HIGH 2 to 4 hours. Serve over spaghetti.

Tip: Recipe can be doubled for a 5-, 6- or 7-quart **CROCK-POT®** slow cooker.

Asian Ginger Beef over Bok Choy

MAKES 6 TO 8 SERVINGS

2 tablespoons peanut oil

1½ pounds boneless beef chuck roast, cut into 1-inch pieces

3 green onions, cut into ½-inch slices

6 cloves garlic

1 cup chicken broth

½ cup water

¼ cup soy sauce

2 teaspoons ground ginger

1 teaspoon Asian chili paste

9 ounces fresh udon noodles or vermicelli, cooked and drained

3 cups bok choy, trimmed, washed and cut into 1-inch pieces

½ cup minced fresh cilantro (optional)

1 Heat oil in large skillet over medium-high heat. Working in batches, brown beef on all sides. Brown last batch of beef with green onions and garlic.

2 Remove to **CROCK-POT**® slow cooker. Add broth, water, soy sauce, ginger and chili paste; stir to blend. Cover; cook on LOW 7 to 8 hours or on HIGH 3 to 4 hours or until beef is very tender.

3 Just before serving, add noodles and bok choy to **CROCK-POT**® slow cooker; stir to blend. Cover; cook on HIGH 15 minutes or until bok choy is tender-crisp. Garnish with cilantro.

Easy Salisbury Steak

MAKES 4 SERVINGS

1	**medium onion, sliced**
1½	**pounds ground beef**
1	**egg**
½	**cup seasoned dry bread crumbs**
2	**teaspoons Worcestershire sauce, divided**
1	**teaspoon dry mustard**
1	**can (10½ ounces) cream of mushroom soup**
½	**cup water**
3	**tablespoons ketchup**
	Chopped fresh Italian parsley (optional)
	Mashed potatoes (optional)
	Steamed peas (optional)

1 Coat inside of **CROCK-POT®** slow cooker with nonstick cooking spray. Layer onion on bottom of **CROCK-POT®** slow cooker.

2 Combine beef, egg, bread crumbs, 1 teaspoon Worcestershire sauce and mustard in large bowl. Form into four 1-inch-thick oval patties. Heat large nonstick skillet over medium-high heat. Add patties; cook 2 minutes per side or until lightly browned. Remove to **CROCK-POT®** slow cooker. Stir soup, water, ketchup and remaining 1 teaspoon Worcestershire sauce in medium bowl. Pour mixture over patties; top with mushrooms. Cover; cook on LOW 3 to 3½ hours. Garnish with parsley. Serve with potatoes and peas, if desired.

Easy Beef Burgundy

MAKES 4 TO 6 SERVINGS

1½ pounds boneless beef round steak, cut into 1-inch pieces

1 can (10¾ ounces) condensed cream of mushroom soup, undiluted

1 cup dry red wine

1 onion, chopped

1 can (4 ounces) sliced mushrooms, drained

1 package (about 1 ounce) dry onion soup mix

1 tablespoon minced garlic

Hot cooked egg noodles (optional)

Combine beef, mushroom soup, wine, onion, mushrooms, dry soup mix and garlic in **CROCK-POT®** slow cooker. Cover; cook on LOW 6 to 8 hours or until beef is tender. Serve over noodles, if desired.

Best Ever Chili

MAKES 8 SERVINGS

1½ **pounds ground beef**

1 **cup chopped onion**

2 **cans (about 15 ounces** *each***) kidney beans, drained and liquid reserved**

1½ **pounds plum tomatoes, diced**

1 **can (15 ounces) tomato paste**

3 **to 6 tablespoons chili powder**

Sour cream and chopped green onion (optional)

1 Brown beef and onion in large skillet 6 to 8 minutes over medium-high heat, stirring to break up meat. Drain fat. Remove beef mixture to **CROCK-POT**® slow cooker with slotted spoon.

2 Add beans, tomatoes, tomato paste, 1 cup reserved bean liquid and chili powder to **CROCK-POT**® slow cooker; mix well. Cover; cook on LOW 10 to 12 hours. Top each serving with sour cream and green onions, if desired.

Braised Chipotle Beef

MAKES 4 TO 6 SERVINGS

3 pounds boneless beef chuck roast, cut into 2-inch pieces

1½ teaspoons salt, plus additional for seasoning

½ teaspoon black pepper, plus additional for seasoning

3 tablespoons vegetable oil, divided

1 large onion, cut into 1-inch pieces

2 red bell peppers, cut into 1-inch pieces

3 tablespoons tomato paste

1 tablespoon minced garlic

1 tablespoon chipotle chili powder*

1 tablespoon paprika

1 tablespoon ground cumin

1 teaspoon dried oregano

1 cup beef broth

1 can (about 14 ounces) diced tomatoes, drained

Hot cooked rice

*Or substitute conventional chili powder.

1 Pat beef dry with paper towels and season with salt and black pepper. Heat 2 tablespoons oil in large skillet over medium-high heat. Working in batches, cook beef in skillet, turning to brown all sides. Remove each batch to **CROCK-POT**® slow cooker as it is finished.

2 Return skillet to medium-high heat. Add remaining 1 tablespoon oil. Add onion; cook and stir just until softened. Add bell peppers; cook 2 minutes. Stir in tomato paste, garlic, chili powder, paprika, cumin, 1½ teaspoons salt, oregano and ½ teaspoon black pepper; cook and stir 1 minute. Remove to **CROCK-POT**® slow cooker.

3 Return skillet to heat; add broth. Cook, stirring to scrape up any browned bits from bottom of skillet. Pour over beef in **CROCK-POT**® slow cooker. Stir in tomatoes. Cover; cook on LOW 7 hours. Turn off heat. Let cooking liquid stand 5 minutes. Skim off and discard fat. Serve beef over rice with cooking liquid.

Beefy Tortellini

MAKES 6 SERVINGS

½ pound ground beef

1 jar (24 to 26 ounces) roasted tomato and garlic pasta sauce

1 package (12 ounces) uncooked three-cheese tortellini

8 ounces sliced button or exotic mushrooms, such as oyster, shiitake and cremini

½ cup water

½ teaspoon red pepper flakes (optional)

¾ cup grated Asiago or Romano cheese

Chopped fresh Italian parsley (optional)

1 Coat inside of **CROCK-POT**® slow cooker with nonstick cooking spray. Brown beef in large skillet over medium-high heat 6 to 8 minutes, stirring to break up meat. Remove to **CROCK-POT**® slow cooker using slotted spoon.

2 Stir pasta sauce, tortellini, mushrooms, water and red pepper flakes, if desired, into **CROCK-POT**® slow cooker. Cover; cook on LOW 2 hours or on HIGH 1 hour. Stir.

3 Cover; cook on LOW 2 to 2½ hours or on HIGH ½ to 1 hour. Serve in shallow bowls topped with cheese and parsley, if desired.

Asian Beef with Mandarin Oranges

MAKES 6 SERVINGS

- **2 tablespoons vegetable oil**
- **2 pounds boneless beef chuck roast, cut into ½-inch strips**
- **1 onion, thinly sliced**
- **1 head bok choy, chopped**
- **1 green bell pepper, sliced**
- **1 can (5 ounces) sliced water chestnuts, drained**
- **1 package (about 3 ounces) shiitake mushrooms, sliced**
- **⅓ cup soy sauce**
- **2 teaspoons minced fresh ginger**
- **¼ teaspoon salt**
- **1 can (11 ounces) mandarin oranges, drained and syrup reserved**
- **2 tablespoons cornstarch**
- **2 cups beef broth**
- **6 cups steamed rice**

1 Heat oil in large skillet over medium-high heat. Working in batches, brown beef on all sides. Remove to **CROCK-POT®** slow cooker.

2 Place onion in skillet; cook and stir over medium heat until softened. Add bok choy, bell pepper, water chestnuts, mushrooms, soy sauce, ginger and salt; cook and stir 5 minutes or until bok choy is wilted. Remove to **CROCK-POT®** slow cooker.

3 Stir reserved mandarin orange syrup into cornstarch in medium bowl until smooth. Whisk into broth in large bowl; pour into **CROCK-POT®** slow cooker. Cover; cook on LOW 10 hours or on HIGH 5 to 6 hours or until beef is tender.

4 Stir in mandarin oranges. Spoon over rice in shallow serving bowls.

Beef and Beet Borscht

MAKES 6 TO 8 SERVINGS

6 slices bacon

1 boneless beef chuck roast
(1½ pounds), trimmed and
cut into ½-inch pieces

1 medium onion, sliced

4 cloves garlic, minced

4 medium beets, peeled and
cut into ½-inch pieces

2 large carrots, sliced

3 cups beef broth

6 sprigs fresh dill

3 tablespoons honey

3 tablespoons red wine
vinegar

2 whole bay leaves

3 cups shredded green
cabbage

1 Heat large skillet over medium heat. Add bacon; cook and stir until crisp. Remove to paper towel-lined plate using slotted spoon; crumble.

2 Return skillet to medium-high heat. Add beef; cook 5 minutes or until browned. Remove beef to **CROCK-POT®** slow cooker.

3 Pour off all but 1 tablespoon fat from skillet. Add onion and garlic; cook 4 minutes or until onion is softened. Remove onion mixture to **CROCK-POT®** slow cooker. Stir in bacon, beets, carrots, broth, dill, honey, vinegar and bay leaves.

4 Cover; cook on LOW 5 to 6 hours. Stir in cabbage. Cover; cook on LOW 30 minutes. Remove and discard bay leaves before serving.

Classic Beef Stew

MAKES 8 SERVINGS

2½ pounds cubed beef stew
   meat

¼ cup all-purpose flour

2 tablespoons olive oil, divided

3 cups beef broth

16 baby carrots

8 fingerling potatoes, halved
   crosswise

1 medium onion, chopped

1 ounce dried oyster
   mushrooms, chopped

2 teaspoons garlic powder

1 teaspoon dried basil

1 teaspoon dried oregano

½ teaspoon dried rosemary

½ teaspoon dried marjoram

½ teaspoon dried sage

½ teaspoon dried thyme

Salt and black pepper
   (optional)

Chopped fresh Italian
   parsley (optional)

1 Combine beef and flour in large bowl; toss well to coat. Heat 1 tablespoon oil in large skillet over medium-high heat. Add half of beef; cook and stir 4 minutes or until browned. Remove to **CROCK-POT®** slow cooker. Repeat with remaining oil and beef.

2 Add broth, carrots, potatoes, onion, mushrooms, garlic powder, basil, oregano, rosemary, marjoram, sage and thyme to **CROCK-POT®** slow cooker; stir to blend. Cover; cook on LOW 10 to 12 hours or on HIGH 5 to 6 hours. Season with salt and pepper, if desired. Garnish with parsley.

Delicious Pepper Steak

MAKES 8 SERVINGS

2 **tablespoons toasted sesame oil**

2 **pounds boneless beef round steak, cut into strips**

½ **medium red bell pepper, sliced**

½ **medium green bell pepper, sliced**

½ **medium yellow bell pepper, sliced**

1 **medium onion, sliced**

14 **grape tomatoes**

⅓ **cup hoisin sauce**

¼ **cup water**

3 **tablespoons all-purpose flour**

3 **tablespoons soy sauce**

2 **teaspoons garlic powder**

1 **teaspoon ground cumin**

1 **teaspoon dried oregano**

1 **teaspoon paprika**

⅛ **teaspoon ground red pepper**

Hot cooked rice (optional)

1 Heat oil in large skillet over medium-high heat. Add beef in batches; cook 4 to 5 minutes or until browned. Remove to large paper towel-lined plate.

2 Add bell peppers, onion and tomatoes to **CROCK-POT®** slow cooker. Combine hoisin sauce, water, flour, soy sauce, garlic powder, cumin, oregano, paprika and ground red pepper in medium bowl; stir to blend. Add to **CROCK-POT®** slow cooker. Add beef. Cover; cook on LOW 8 to 9 hours or on HIGH 4 to 4½ hours. Serve with rice, if desired.

Simple Beef Chili

MAKES 8 SERVINGS

3 pounds ground beef

2 cans (about 14 ounces *each*) unsalted diced tomatoes

2 cans (about 15 ounces *each*) kidney beans, rinsed and drained

2 cups chopped onions

1 package (10 ounces) frozen corn

1 cup chopped green bell pepper

1 can (8 ounces) tomato sauce

3 tablespoons chili powder

1 teaspoon garlic powder

½ teaspoon ground cumin

½ teaspoon dried oregano

1 Brown beef in large skillet over medium-high heat 6 to 8 minutes, stirring to break up meat. Remove to **CROCK-POT**® slow cooker using slotted spoon.

2 Add tomatoes, beans, onions, corn, bell pepper, tomato sauce, chili powder, garlic powder, cumin and oregano to **CROCK-POT**® slow cooker. Cover; cook on LOW 4 hours.

Tip: The flavor and aroma of herbs and spices may lessen during a longer cooking time. So, when slow cooking in your **CROCK-POT**® slow cooker, be sure to taste and adjust seasonings before serving.

Greek-Style Meatballs and Spinach

MAKES 4 SERVINGS

½	cup old-fashioned oats
¼	cup minced onion
1	clove garlic, minced
¼	teaspoon dried oregano
⅛	teaspoon black pepper
1	egg
8	ounces ground lamb

1	cup beef broth
¼	teaspoon salt
½	cup plain nonfat yogurt
1	teaspoon all-purpose flour
4	cups fresh baby spinach, coarsely chopped
1⅓	cups hot cooked egg noodles

1 Combine oats, onion, garlic, oregano and pepper in medium bowl; stir in egg. Add lamb; mix well but do not knead. Shape mixture into 16 balls. Place in **CROCK-POT®** slow cooker. Add broth and salt. Cover; cook on LOW 6 hours.

2 Stir yogurt into flour in small bowl. Spoon about ¼ cup hot liquid from **CROCK-POT®** slow cooker into yogurt mixture; stir until smooth. Whisk yogurt mixture into **CROCK-POT®** slow cooker. Add spinach. Cover; cook on LOW 10 minutes or until heated through. Serve over noodles.

Corn Chip Chili

MAKES 6 SERVINGS

1 tablespoon olive oil

1 medium onion, chopped

1 medium red bell pepper, chopped

1 jalapeño pepper, seeded and finely chopped*

4 cloves garlic, minced

2 pounds ground beef

1 can (4 ounces) diced mild green chiles, drained

2 cans (about 14 ounces each) fire-roasted diced tomatoes

2 tablespoons chili powder

1½ teaspoons ground cumin

1½ teaspoons dried oregano

¾ teaspoon salt

3 cups corn chips

1 cup (4 ounces) shredded sharp Cheddar cheese

6 tablespoons chopped green onions

*Jalapeño peppers can sting and irritate the skin, so wear rubber gloves when handling peppers and do not touch your eyes.

1 Coat inside of **CROCK-POT®** slow cooker with nonstick cooking spray.

2 Heat oil in large skillet over medium-high heat. Add onion, bell pepper, jalapeño pepper and garlic; cook and stir 2 minutes or until softened. Add beef; cook and stir 10 to 12 minutes or until beef is no longer pink and liquid has evaporated. Stir in green chiles; cook 1 minute. Remove beef mixture to **CROCK-POT®** slow cooker using slotted spoon. Stir in tomatoes, chili powder, cumin and oregano.

3 Cover; cook on LOW 6 to 7 hours or on HIGH 3½ to 4 hours. Stir in salt. Place corn chips evenly into serving bowls; top with chili. Sprinkle with cheese and green onions.

PORK PLEASERS

Chili Verde

MAKES 4 SERVINGS

Nonstick cooking spray

¾ pound boneless lean pork, cut into 1-inch cubes

1 pound fresh tomatillos, husks removed, rinsed and coarsely chopped

1 can (about 15 ounces) cannellini beans, rinsed and drained

1 can (about 14 ounces) chicken broth

1 large onion, halved and thinly sliced

1 can (4 ounces) diced mild green chiles

6 cloves garlic, sliced

1 teaspoon ground cumin

Salt and black pepper

½ cup lightly packed fresh cilantro, chopped

1 Spray large skillet with cooking spray. Heat over medium-high heat. Add pork; cook 6 to 8 minutes or until browned on all sides.

2 Combine pork, tomatillos, beans, broth, onion, chiles, garlic, cumin, salt and pepper in **CROCK-POT**® slow cooker. Cover; cook on HIGH 3 to 4 hours. Stir in cilantro.

Golden Harvest Pork Stew

MAKES 4 SERVINGS

1 pound boneless pork cutlets, cut into 1-inch pieces

2 tablespoons all-purpose flour, divided

1 tablespoon vegetable oil

2 medium Yukon Gold potatoes, unpeeled and cut into 1-inch cubes

1 large sweet potato, cut into 1-inch cubes

1 cup chopped carrots

1 ear corn, broken into 4 pieces or ½ cup corn

½ cup chicken broth

1 jalapeño pepper, seeded and finely chopped*

1 clove garlic, minced

1 teaspoon salt

¼ teaspoon black pepper

¼ teaspoon dried thyme

Chopped fresh Italian parsley (optional)

*Jalapeño peppers can sting and irritate the skin, so wear rubber gloves when handling peppers and do not touch your eyes.

1 Toss pork pieces with 1 tablespoon flour in large bowl; set aside. Heat oil in large skillet over medium-high heat. Add pork; cook 6 to 8 minutes or until browned on all sides. Remove to **CROCK-POT®** slow cooker.

2 Add potatoes, carrots, corn, broth, jalapeño pepper, garlic, salt, black pepper and thyme; stir to blend. Cover; cook on LOW 5 to 6 hours.

3 Stir ¼ cup cooking liquid into remaining 1 tablespoon flour in small bowl until smooth; whisk into **CROCK-POT®** slow cooker. Turn **CROCK-POT®** slow cooker to HIGH. Cover; cook on HIGH 10 minutes or until thickened. Garnish with parsley.

Saucy Pork Loin and Potatoes

MAKES 6 SERVINGS

- **1** tablespoon olive oil
- **1** pork tenderloin (2 pounds)
- **½** cup chicken broth
- **3** tablespoons cornstarch
- **½** cup packed brown sugar
- **⅓** cup soy sauce
- **¼** cup lemon juice
- **¼** cup dry white wine

- **2** cloves garlic, minced
- **1** tablespoon dry mustard
- **1** tablespoon Worcestershire sauce
- **3** cups Russet potatoes, unpeeled and cut into wedges

  Chopped fresh Italian parsley (optional)

1 Heat oil in large skillet over medium-high heat. Brown pork tenderloin 4 to 6 minutes on each side. Stir broth into cornstarch in small bowl until smooth. Place pork, broth mixture, brown sugar, soy sauce, lemon juice, wine, garlic, mustard and Worcestershire sauce in **CROCK-POT®** slow cooker. Cover; cook on LOW 4 hours.

2 Stir potatoes into **CROCK-POT®** slow cooker; turn tenderloin. Cover; cook on LOW 2 hours. Garnish with parsley.

Pork Soup with Soba Noodles and Bok Choy

MAKES 6 TO 8 SERVINGS

2 tablespoons olive oil

1 boneless pork loin roast (about 2½ pounds), cut into matchstick pieces

2 tablespoons hoisin sauce

1 tablespoon sugar

1 to 2 teaspoons Chinese five-spice powder

6 cups chicken broth

1½ tablespoons fresh ginger, peeled and cut into thin slices

3 cloves garlic, thinly sliced

2 tablespoons soy sauce

1 head bok choy, sliced

1 pound soba noodles, cooked

1 Heat oil in large skillet. Add pork, hoisin sauce, sugar and five-spice powder; cook and stir 5 to 7 minutes or until pork is browned. Remove pork mixture to **CROCK-POT**® slow cooker.

2 Add broth, ginger, garlic, soy sauce and bok choy to **CROCK-POT**® slow cooker. Cover; cook on LOW 6 to 7 hours or on HIGH 3 to 4 hours.

3 Stir in soba noodles. Cover; cook on HIGH 10 minutes or until just heated through.

Braised Pork Shanks with Israeli Couscous and Root Vegetable Stew

MAKES 4 SERVINGS

4 **pork shanks, bone in, skin removed (about 1½ pounds total)**

Coarse salt and black pepper

1 **cup olive oil**

4 **large carrots, sliced diagonally into 1-inch pieces and divided**

4 **stalks celery, sliced diagonally into 1-inch pieces and divided**

1 **Spanish onion, peeled and quartered**

4 **cloves garlic, crushed**

4 **to 6 cups chicken broth**

2 **cups dry white wine**

¼ **cup tomato paste**

¼ **cup distilled white vinegar**

1 **tablespoon whole black peppercorns**

Israeli couscous (recipe follows)

1. Season shanks well with salt and black pepper. Heat oil in large skillet over medium heat. Add shanks; cook 7 to 10 minutes or until browned on all sides. Remove to **CROCK-POT®** slow cooker.

2. Pour off all but 2 tablespoons oil in skillet. Add half of carrots, half of celery, onion and garlic to skillet; cook and stir 5 minutes or until vegetables are soft but not brown. Remove to **CROCK-POT®** slow cooker.

3. Add broth, wine, tomato paste, vinegar and peppercorns to skillet. Bring to a boil, stirring and scraping up any browned bits from bottom of skillet. Pour over shanks. Cover; cook on HIGH 2 hours, turning shanks every 20 minutes.

4. Remove shanks to large bowl. Strain cooking liquid; discard solids. Return cooking liquid to **CROCK-POT®** slow cooker. Add remaining carrots and celery. Return shanks to **CROCK-POT®** slow cooker. Cover; cook on HIGH 1 hour.

5. Meanwhile, prepare Israeli Couscous.

6 Add Israeli Couscous to **CROCK-POT**® slow cooker. Cover; cook on HIGH 10 minutes or until heated through. Place Israeli Couscous, carrots and celery in shallow bowls. Place shank on top; spoon cooking liquid into each bowl.

Israeli Couscous

MAKES ABOUT 2 CUPS

2   **cups water**

Pinch salt

1⅓   **cups Israeli or regular couscous**

Place water and salt in large skillet over medium-low heat; bring to a boil over high heat. Add couscous; cook and stir 6 to 8 minutes or until tender. Rinse and drain under cold water.

Stew Provençal

MAKES 8 SERVINGS

2	**cans (about 14 ounces** *each***) beef broth, divided**
⅓	**cup all-purpose flour**
1	**to 2 pork tenderloins (about 2 pounds** *each***), trimmed and diced**
4	**red potatoes, unpeeled and cut into cubes**
2	**cups frozen cut green beans, thawed**
1	**onion, chopped**
2	**cloves garlic, minced**
1	**teaspoon salt**
1	**teaspoon dried thyme**
½	**teaspoon black pepper**
	Sprigs fresh thyme (optional)

1 Combine ¾ cup beef broth and flour in small bowl; cover and refrigerate. Add remaining broth, pork, potatoes, beans, onion, garlic, salt, dried thyme and pepper to **CROCK-POT**® slow cooker; mix well. Cover; cook on LOW 8 to 10 hours or on HIGH 4 to 5 hours.

2 Whisk flour mixture into **CROCK-POT**® slow cooker. Cook, uncovered, on HIGH 30 minutes or until thickened. Garnish with thyme sprigs.

Jerk Pork and Sweet Potato Stew

MAKES 4 SERVINGS

1¼ pounds boneless pork shoulder roast, cut into 1-inch pieces

2 tablespoons all-purpose flour

¼ teaspoon salt

¼ teaspoon black pepper

2 tablespoons vegetable oil

1 large sweet potato, diced

1 cup frozen or canned corn

¼ cup minced green onions (green parts only), divided

1 clove garlic, minced

½ medium Scotch bonnet pepper or jalapeño pepper, seeded and minced (about 1 teaspoon)*

⅛ teaspoon ground allspice

1 cup chicken broth

1 tablespoon lime juice

2 cups cooked rice (optional)

*Scotch bonnet and jalapeño peppers can sting and irritate the skin, so wear rubber gloves when handling peppers and do not touch your eyes.

1 Combine pork, flour, salt and black pepper in large resealable food storage bag; seal bag. Shake to coat. Heat oil in large skillet over medium heat. Add pork in batches; cook 5 minutes or until browned. Remove to **CROCK-POT®** slow cooker.

2 Stir in sweet potato, corn, 2 tablespoons green onions, garlic, Scotch bonnet pepper and allspice. Stir in broth. Cover; cook on LOW 5 to 6 hours.

3 Stir in lime juice and remaining 2 tablespoons green onions. Top stew with rice, if desired.

Hearty Pork and Bacon Chili

MAKES 8 TO 10 SERVINGS

2½ pounds boneless pork shoulder roast, cut into 1-inch pieces

3½ teaspoons salt, divided

1¼ teaspoons black pepper, divided

1 tablespoon vegetable oil

4 slices thick-cut bacon, diced

2 medium onions, chopped

1 red bell pepper, chopped

¼ cup chili powder

2 tablespoons tomato paste

1 tablespoon minced garlic

1 tablespoon ground cumin

1 tablespoon smoked paprika

1 bottle (12 ounces) pale ale

2 cans (about 14 ounces each) diced tomatoes

2 cups water

¾ cup dried kidney beans, rinsed and sorted

¾ cup dried black beans, rinsed and sorted

3 tablespoons cornmeal

Feta cheese and chopped fresh cilantro (optional)

1 Season pork with 1 teaspoon salt and 1 teaspoon black pepper. Heat oil in large skillet over medium-high heat. Cook pork in batches 6 minutes or until browned on all sides. Remove to **CROCK-POT**® slow cooker using slotted spoon.

2 Heat same skillet over medium heat. Add bacon; cook and stir until crisp. Remove to **CROCK-POT**® slow cooker using slotted spoon.

3 Pour off all but 2 tablespoons fat from skillet. Return skillet to medium heat. Add onions and bell pepper; cook and stir 6 minutes or just until softened. Stir in chili powder, tomato paste, garlic, cumin, paprika, remaining 2½ teaspoons salt and remaining ¼ teaspoon black pepper; cook and stir 1 minute. Stir in ale. Bring to a simmer, scraping up any browned bits from bottom of skillet. Pour over pork in **CROCK-POT**® slow cooker. Stir in tomatoes, water, beans and cornmeal.

4 Cover; cook on LOW 10 hours. Turn off heat. Let stand 10 minutes. Skim fat from surface. Garnish each serving with cheese and cilantro.

Mango Ginger Pork Roast

MAKES 4 TO 6 SERVINGS

1 boneless pork shoulder roast (about 4 pounds)*

½ to 1 teaspoon ground ginger

Salt and black pepper

2 cups mango salsa

2 tablespoons honey

¼ cup apricot preserves

Hot cooked rice

*Unless you have a 5-, 6- or 7-quart CROCK-POT® slow cooker, cut any roast larger than 2½ pounds in half so it cooks completely.

1 Season roast with ginger, salt and pepper. Add to **CROCK-POT®** slow cooker.

2 Combine salsa, honey and preserves in medium bowl; stir to blend. Pour over roast. Cover; cook on LOW 6 to 8 hours.

3 Turn **CROCK-POT®** slow cooker to HIGH. Cover; cook on HIGH 3 to 4 hours or until roast is tender. Serve with rice.

Asian Noodles with Pork and Vegetables

MAKES 6 SERVINGS

¾ **cup soy sauce**

¾ **cup honey**

4 **cloves garlic, chopped**

1 **tablespoon ground ginger**

1 **boneless pork shoulder roast (2½ pounds), trimmed**

¾ **cup Asian sweet chili sauce**

¼ **cup water**

3 **tablespoons cornstarch**

2 **packages (16 ounces each) frozen mixed Asian vegetables**

1 **tablespoon toasted sesame oil**

Hot cooked soba noodles or rice

1 Mix soy sauce, honey, garlic and ginger in **CROCK-POT®** slow cooker. Add pork. Cover; cook on LOW 8 to 10 hours or on HIGH 5 to 6 hours or until pork is fork-tender. Remove pork to large cutting board.

2 Stir chili sauce into **CROCK-POT®** slow cooker. Stir water into cornstarch in small bowl until smooth; whisk into **CROCK-POT®** slow cooker. Cover; cook on HIGH 15 minutes or until thickened. Meanwhile, shred pork with two forks.

3 Add vegetables and shredded pork to **CROCK-POT®** slow cooker. Cover; cook on HIGH 10 to 20 minutes. Stir in oil. Serve over soba noodles.

Pozole Rojo

MAKES 8 SERVINGS

4 dried ancho chiles, stemmed and seeded

3 dried guajillo chiles, stemmed and seeded*

2 cups boiling water

2½ pounds boneless pork shoulder roast, trimmed and cut in half

3 teaspoons salt, divided

1 tablespoon vegetable oil

2 medium onions, chopped

1½ tablespoons minced garlic

2 teaspoons ground cumin

2 teaspoons Mexican oregano**

4 cups chicken broth

2 cans (30 ounces each) white hominy, rinsed and drained

Optional toppings: sliced radishes, lime wedges, sliced romaine lettuce, chopped onion, tortilla chips and/or diced avocado

Guajillo chiles can be found in the ethnic section of large supermarkets.

**Mexican oregano has a stronger flavor than regular oregano. It can be found in the spices and seasonings section of most large supermarkets.*

1 Place ancho and guajillo chiles in medium bowl; pour boiling water over top. Weigh down chiles with small plate or bowl; soak 30 minutes.

2 Meanwhile, season pork with 1 teaspoon salt. Heat oil in large skillet over medium-high heat. Add pork; cook 8 to 10 minutes or until browned on all sides. Remove to **CROCK-POT®** slow cooker.

3 Heat same skillet over medium heat. Add onions; cook 6 minutes or until softened. Add garlic, cumin, oregano and remaining 2 teaspoons salt; cook and stir 1 minute. Stir in broth; bring to a simmer, scraping up any browned bits from bottom of skillet. Pour over pork in **CROCK-POT®** slow cooker.

4 Place softened chiles and soaking liquid in food processor or blender; blend until smooth. Pour through fine-mesh sieve into medium bowl, pressing with spoon to extract liquid. Discard solids. Stir mixture into **CROCK-POT®** slow cooker.

5 Cover; cook on LOW 5 hours. Stir in hominy. Cover; cook on LOW 1 hour. Turn off heat. Let stand 10 to 15 minutes. Skim off fat and discard. Remove pork to large cutting board; shred with two forks. Ladle hominy mixture into bowls; top each serving with pork and desired toppings.

Spiced Pork and Apple Stew

MAKES 8 SERVINGS

1 teaspoon canola oil

1¼ pounds cubed lean pork stew meat

1 medium sweet onion, cut into ½-inch-thick slices

2 cloves garlic, minced

1 can (28 ounces) crushed tomatoes

2 large or 3 small red or white potatoes, cut into 1-inch pieces

1½ cups baby carrots, cut into ½-inch pieces

2 small apples, cored and cubed

1 cup chicken broth

2 tablespoons spicy brown mustard

1 tablespoon packed brown sugar

2 teaspoons ground cinnamon

1 teaspoon ground cumin

¼ teaspoon salt

2 tablespoons chopped fresh Italian parsley (optional)

1 Heat oil in large skillet over medium-high heat. Add pork; cook 6 to 8 minutes or until browned on all sides. Add onion and garlic; cook and stir 5 minutes. Remove to **CROCK-POT®** slow cooker.

2 Add tomatoes, potatoes, carrots, apples, broth, mustard, brown sugar, cinnamon, cumin and salt to **CROCK-POT®** slow cooker; stir to blend. Cover; cook on LOW 6 to 8 hours or until pork and potatoes are tender. Garnish with parsley.

Country Sausage and Bean Soup

MAKES 9 SERVINGS

Nonstick cooking spray

6 ounces bulk pork sausage

2 cans (about 14 ounces *each*)
chicken broth

1½ cups hot water

1 cup dried black beans, rinsed
and sorted

1 cup chopped onion

2 whole bay leaves

1 teaspoon sugar

⅛ teaspoon ground red pepper

1 cup chopped tomato

1 tablespoon chili powder

1 tablespoon Worcestershire
sauce

2 teaspoons extra virgin olive
oil

1½ teaspoons ground cumin

½ teaspoon salt

¼ cup chopped fresh cilantro
(optional)

1 Spray large skillet with cooking spray; heat over medium-high heat. Add sausage; cook 6 to 8 minutes or until beginning to brown, stirring to break up meat.

2 Combine broth, water, beans, onion, bay leaves, sugar and ground red pepper in **CROCK-POT®** slow cooker; stir to blend. Cover; cook on LOW 8 hours or on HIGH 4 hours.

3 Add tomato, chili powder, Worcestershire sauce, oil, cumin and salt to **CROCK-POT®** slow cooker; stir to blend. Cover; cook on HIGH 15 minutes or until heated through. Garnish with cilantro.

Sweet and Spicy Pork Picadillo

MAKES 4 SERVINGS

1 tablespoon olive oil

1 yellow onion, cut into ¼-inch pieces

2 cloves garlic, minced

1 pound boneless pork country-style ribs, trimmed and cut into 1-inch cubes

1 can (about 14 ounces) diced tomatoes

3 tablespoons cider vinegar

2 canned chipotle peppers in adobo sauce, chopped*

½ cup raisins

½ teaspoon ground cumin

½ teaspoon ground cinnamon

Hot cooked rice (optional)

Black beans (optional)

*You may substitute dried chipotle peppers, soaked in warm water about 20 minutes to soften before chopping.

1 Heat oil in large skillet over medium-low heat. Add onion and garlic; cook and stir 4 minutes. Add pork; cook and stir 5 to 7 minutes or until browned. Remove to **CROCK-POT®** slow cooker.

2 Combine tomatoes, vinegar, chipotle peppers, raisins, cumin and cinnamon in medium bowl; stir to blend. Pour over pork in **CROCK-POT®** slow cooker. Cover; cook on LOW 5 hours or on HIGH 3 hours. Remove pork to large cutting board; shred with two forks. Serve with rice and beans, if desired.

Pork Tenderloin Chili

MAKES 8 SERVINGS

1½ to 2 pounds pork tenderloin, cooked and cut into 2-inch pieces

2 cans (about 15 ounces each) pinto beans, rinsed and drained

2 cans (about 15 ounces each) black beans, rinsed and drained

2 cans (about 14 ounces each) whole tomatoes

2 cans (4 ounces each) diced mild green chiles

1 package (1¼ ounces) taco seasoning mix

Diced avocado (optional)

Combine pork, beans, tomatoes, chiles and taco seasoning mix in **CROCK-POT**® slow cooker; stir to blend. Cover; cook on LOW 4 hours. Top with avocado, if desired.

VEGETARIAN FAVORITES

Chipotle Vegetable Chili with Chocolate

MAKES 6 SERVINGS

2 tablespoons olive oil

1 medium onion, chopped

1 medium green bell pepper, chopped

1 medium red bell pepper, chopped

1 cup frozen corn

1 can (28 ounces) diced tomatoes

1 can (about 15 ounces) black beans, rinsed and drained

1 can (about 15 ounces) pinto beans, rinsed and drained

1 tablespoon chili powder

1 teaspoon ground cumin

½ teaspoon chipotle chili powder

1 ounce semisweet chocolate, chopped

1 Heat oil in large skillet over medium-high heat. Add onion and bell peppers; cook and stir 4 minutes or until softened. Stir in corn; cook 3 minutes. Remove to **CROCK-POT**® slow cooker.

2 Stir tomatoes, beans, chili powder, cumin and chipotle chili powder into **CROCK-POT**® slow cooker. Cover; cook on LOW 6 to 7 hours. Stir chocolate into **CROCK-POT**® slow cooker until melted.

Chickpea and Vegetable Curry

MAKES 4 SERVINGS

1 can (about 13 ounces) unsweetened coconut milk

1 cup vegetable broth, divided

2 teaspoons curry powder

¼ teaspoon ground red pepper

2 cups cut fresh green beans, cut into 1-inch pieces

1 can (about 15 ounces) chickpeas, rinsed and drained

2 carrots, very thinly sliced

½ cup golden raisins

¼ cup all-purpose flour

2 cups hot cooked couscous

Green onion and toasted sliced almonds (optional)

1 Coat inside of **CROCK-POT®** slow cooker with nonstick cooking spray. Combine coconut milk, ¾ cup broth, curry powder and ground red pepper in **CROCK-POT®** slow cooker. Stir in green beans, chickpeas, carrots and raisins. Cover; cook on LOW 6 to 7 hours or on HIGH 2½ to 3 hours or until vegetables are tender.

2 Stir remaining ¼ cup broth into flour in small bowl until smooth; whisk into vegetable mixture. Cover; cook on HIGH 15 minutes or until thickened. Ladle into shallow bowls; top with couscous, green onion and almonds, if desired.

Creamy Mushroom Stroganoff

MAKES 4 SERVINGS

3 tablespoons unsalted butter

2 medium onions, sliced

2½ pounds white button mushrooms, thickly sliced and divided

1 teaspoon dried thyme

¾ teaspoon salt, divided

½ teaspoon ground black pepper, divided

6 cloves garlic, minced

⅓ cup dry white wine

1 cup vegetable broth

2 teaspoons Worcestershire sauce

2 teaspoons Dijon mustard

⅔ cup sour cream

2 tablespoons chopped fresh Italian parsley

8 ounces extra wide egg noodles, cooked and drained

1 Coat inside of **CROCK-POT**® slow cooker with nonstick cooking spray. Melt butter in large skillet over medium-high heat. Add onions, half of mushrooms, thyme, ½ teaspoon salt and ¼ teaspoon pepper; cook and stir 3 minutes or until mushrooms have cooked down slightly. Add remaining mushrooms. Cook 15 minutes or until mushrooms are tender and liquid has almost completely evaporated. Add garlic; cook 2 minutes. Pour in wine; cook and stir 1 minute. Remove to **CROCK-POT**® slow cooker. Stir in broth, Worcestershire sauce and mustard.

2 Cover; cook on LOW 4 to 4½ hours or HIGH 2 to 2½ hours. Turn off heat. Let cool 10 minutes. Stir in sour cream, parsley and remaining ¼ teaspoon salt and ¼ teaspoon pepper. Divide noodles evenly among four plates; top with stroganoff to serve.

Thai Red Curry with Tofu

MAKES 4 SERVINGS

1 medium sweet potato, peeled and cut into 1-inch pieces

1 small eggplant, halved lengthwise and cut crosswise into ½-inch-wide halves

8 ounces extra firm tofu, cut into 1-inch pieces

½ cup green beans, cut into 1-inch pieces

½ red bell pepper, cut into ¼-inch-wide strips

2 tablespoons vegetable oil

5 medium shallots (about 1½ cups), thinly sliced

3 tablespoons Thai red curry paste

1 teaspoon minced garlic

1 teaspoon grated fresh ginger

1 can (about 13 ounces) unsweetened coconut milk

1½ tablespoons soy sauce

1 tablespoon packed light brown sugar

¼ cup chopped fresh basil

2 tablespoons lime juice

Hot cooked rice (optional)

1 Coat inside of **CROCK-POT**® slow cooker with nonstick cooking spray. Add potato, eggplant, tofu, beans and bell pepper.

2 Heat oil in large skillet over medium heat. Add shallots; cook 5 minutes or until browned and tender. Add curry paste, garlic and ginger; cook and stir 1 minute. Add coconut milk, soy sauce and brown sugar; bring to a simmer. Pour mixture over vegetables in **CROCK-POT**® slow cooker.

3 Cover; cook on LOW 2 to 3 hours. Stir in basil and lime juice. Serve with rice, if desired.

Farro Risotto with Mushrooms and Spinach

MAKES 4 SERVINGS

2 tablespoons olive oil, divided

1 onion, chopped

12 ounces cremini mushrooms, stems trimmed and quartered

¼ teaspoon black pepper

2 cloves garlic, minced

1 cup uncooked farro

1 sprig fresh thyme

4 cups vegetable broth

8 ounces baby spinach

½ cup grated Parmesan cheese

1 Heat 1 tablespoon oil in large skillet over medium heat. Add onion; cook 8 minutes or until tender. Remove to **CROCK-POT**® slow cooker. Add remaining 1 tablespoon oil to same skillet; heat over medium-high heat. Add mushrooms and pepper; cook 6 to 8 minutes or until mushrooms have released their liquid and are browned. Add garlic; cook 1 minute. Stir in farro and thyme; cook 1 minute. Remove mushroom mixture to **CROCK-POT**® slow cooker.

2 Stir broth into **CROCK-POT**® slow cooker. Cover; cook on HIGH 3½ hours or until farro is tender and broth is absorbed. Remove and discard thyme sprig. Stir in spinach and cheese just before serving.

Sweet Potato and Black Bean Chipotle Chili

MAKES 8 TO 10 SERVINGS

1 tablespoon vegetable oil

2 large onions, diced

1 tablespoon minced garlic

2 tablespoons tomato paste

3 tablespoons chili powder

1 tablespoon chipotle chili powder

1 teaspoon ground cumin

2 teaspoons kosher salt

1 cup water

2 large sweet potatoes, peeled and cut into ½-inch pieces (about 2 pounds)

2 cans (28 ounces each) black beans, rinsed and drained

2 cans (28 ounces each) crushed tomatoes

Optional toppings: sliced green onions, shredded Cheddar cheese and/or tortilla chips

1 Heat oil in large skillet over medium-high heat. Add onions; cook 8 minutes or until lightly browned and softened. Add garlic, tomato paste, chili powder, chipotle chili powder, cumin and salt; cook and stir 1 minute. Add water, stirring to scrape up any brown bits from bottom of skillet. Remove to **CROCK-POT®** slow cooker. Add sweet potatoes, beans and tomatoes.

2 Cover; cook on LOW 8 hours or on HIGH 4 hours. Ladle into individual bowls. Top with desired toppings.

Mushroom and Vegetable Ragoût over Polenta

MAKES 6 SERVINGS

3 tablespoons extra virgin olive oil

8 ounces sliced mushrooms

8 ounces shiitake mushrooms, stemmed and thinly sliced

½ cup Madeira wine

1 can (28 ounces) crushed tomatoes

1 can (about 15 ounces) chickpeas, rinsed and drained

1 medium onion, chopped

1 can (about 6 ounces) tomato paste

4 cloves garlic, minced

1 sprig fresh rosemary

2 cups water

2 cups whole milk

¼ teaspoon salt

2 cups instant polenta

½ cup grated Parmesan cheese

1 Heat oil in large skillet over medium-high heat. Add mushrooms; cook and stir 8 to 10 minutes or until mushrooms are brown. Add Madeira; cook 1 minute or until liquid is reduced by one half. Remove to **CROCK-POT®** slow cooker.

2 Stir crushed tomatoes, chickpeas, onion, tomato paste, garlic and rosemary into **CROCK-POT®** slow cooker. Cover; cook on LOW 6 hours or until vegetables are tender. Remove and discard rosemary.

3 For polenta, combine water, milk and salt in large saucepan over medium-high heat. Bring to a boil; slowly whisk in polenta in slow, steady stream. Cook 4 to 5 minutes, whisking until thick and creamy.

4 Remove polenta from heat; stir in cheese. Top polenta with ragoût.

Asian Sweet Potato and Corn Stew

MAKES 6 SERVINGS

- 1 tablespoon vegetable oil
- 1 large onion, chopped
- 2 tablespoons peeled minced fresh ginger
- ½ jalapeño or serrano pepper, seeded and minced*
- 2 cloves garlic, minced
- 1 cup frozen corn, thawed
- 2 teaspoons curry powder
- 1 can (about 13 ounces) unsweetened coconut milk
- 1 teaspoon cornstarch

- 4 sweet potatoes, cut into ¾-inch cubes
- 1 can (about 14 ounces) vegetable broth
- 1 tablespoon soy sauce

  Hot cooked jasmine or long grain rice

  Optional toppings: chopped fresh cilantro, peanuts and green onions (optional)

Jalapeño and serrano peppers can sting and irritate the skin, so wear rubber gloves when handling peppers and do not touch your eyes.

1 Heat oil in large skillet over medium heat. Add onion, ginger, jalapeño pepper and garlic; cook and stir 5 minutes. Remove from heat. Stir in corn and curry powder.

2 Stir coconut milk into cornstarch in **CROCK-POT®** slow cooker. Stir in potatoes, broth and soy sauce; top with curried corn. Cover; cook on LOW 5 to 6 hours. Stir gently to smooth cooking liquid. Spoon over rice in bowls. Top as desired.

Vegetarian Chili

MAKES 4 SERVINGS

1 tablespoon vegetable oil

1 cup chopped onion

1 cup chopped red bell pepper

2 tablespoons minced jalapeño pepper*

1 clove garlic, minced

1 can (about 28 ounces) stewed tomatoes

1 can (about 15 ounces) black beans, rinsed and drained

1 can (about 15 ounces) chickpeas, rinsed and drained

½ cup frozen corn

¼ cup tomato paste

1 teaspoon sugar

1 teaspoon ground cumin

1 teaspoon dried basil

1 teaspoon chili powder

¼ teaspoon black pepper

*Jalapeño peppers can sting and irritate the skin, so wear rubber gloves when handling peppers and do not touch your eyes.

1 Heat oil in large skillet over medium-high heat. Add onion, bell pepper, jalapeño pepper and garlic; cook and stir 5 minutes. Remove onion mixture to **CROCK-POT®** slow cooker using slotted spoon.

2 Add tomatoes, beans, chickpeas, corn, tomato paste, sugar, cumin, basil, chili powder and black pepper; stir to blend. Cover; cook on LOW 4 to 5 hours.

Koshari

MAKES 6 TO 8 SERVINGS

6 cups water

1 cup uncooked basmati rice, rinsed and drained

1 cup brown lentils, rinsed and sorted

3 teaspoons salt, divided

1 teaspoon ground cinnamon, divided

½ teaspoon ground nutmeg, divided

1 cup uncooked elbow macaroni

4 tablespoons olive oil, divided

1 large onion, thinly sliced

1 large onion, diced

1 tablespoon minced garlic

1 teaspoon ground cumin

½ teaspoon ground coriander

¼ teaspoon red pepper flakes

¼ teaspoon black pepper

1 can (28 ounces) crushed tomatoes

2 teaspoons red wine vinegar

1 Place water, rice, lentils, 2 teaspoons salt, ½ teaspoon cinnamon and ¼ teaspoon nutmeg in **CROCK-POT**® slow cooker. Cover; cook on HIGH 2½ hours. Stir in macaroni. Cover; cook on HIGH 30 minutes, stirring halfway through cooking time.

2 Meanwhile, heat 2 tablespoons oil in large skillet over medium-high heat. Add sliced onion; cook 12 minutes or until edges are dark brown and onion is softened. Remove onions to medium bowl, using slotted spoon. Season with ¼ teaspoon salt. Set aside.

3 Heat same skillet with remaining 2 tablespoons oil over medium heat. Add diced onion; cook 8 minutes or until softened. Add garlic, cumin, coriander, remaining ½ teaspoon cinnamon, red pepper flakes, black pepper and remaining ¼ teaspoon nutmeg; cook 30 seconds or until fragrant. Stir in tomatoes and remaining ¾ teaspoon salt; cook 8 to 10 minutes or until thickened, stirring occasionally. Stir in vinegar.

4 Fluff rice mixture lightly before scooping into individual bowls. Top each serving evenly with tomato sauce and reserved onions.

Mexican Hot Pot

MAKES 6 SERVINGS

1 tablespoon canola oil

1 medium onion, chopped

3 cloves garlic, minced

2 teaspoons red pepper flakes

2 teaspoons dried oregano

1 teaspoon ground cumin

1 can (28 ounces) whole tomatoes, drained and chopped

2 cups corn

1 can (about 15 ounces) chickpeas, rinsed and drained

1 can (about 15 ounces) pinto beans, rinsed and drained

1 cup water

6 cups shredded iceberg lettuce

1 Heat oil in large skillet over medium-high heat. Add onion and garlic; cook and stir 5 minutes. Add red pepper flakes, oregano and cumin; mix well.

2 Remove onion mixture to **CROCK-POT®** slow cooker. Stir in tomatoes, corn, chickpeas, beans and water. Cover; cook on LOW 7 to 8 hours or on HIGH 2 to 3 hours. Top each serving with 1 cup shredded lettuce.

Roasted Summer Squash with Pine Nuts and Romano Cheese

MAKES 6 TO 8 SERVINGS

2 tablespoons olive oil

½ cup chopped yellow onion

1 medium red bell pepper, chopped

1 clove garlic, minced

3 medium zucchini, cut into ½-inch slices

3 medium summer squash, cut into ½-inch slices

½ cup chopped pine nuts

⅓ cup grated Romano cheese

1 teaspoon Italian seasoning

1 teaspoon salt

¼ teaspoon black pepper

1 tablespoon unsalted butter, cubed

Sprigs fresh basil (optional)

1 Heat oil in large skillet over medium-high heat. Add onion, bell pepper and garlic; cook and stir 10 minutes or until onion is translucent and soft. Remove to **CROCK-POT**® slow cooker. Add zucchini and summer squash; toss lightly.

2 Combine pine nuts, cheese, Italian seasoning, salt and black pepper in small bowl. Fold half of pine nut mixture into zucchini. Sprinkle remaining cheese mixture on top. Dot with butter. Cover; cook on LOW 4 to 6 hours. Garnish with basil.

Slow-Cooked Shakshuka

MAKES 6 SERVINGS

¼ cup extra virgin olive oil

1 medium onion, chopped

1 large red bell pepper, chopped

3 cloves garlic, sliced

1 can (28 ounces) crushed tomatoes with basil, garlic and oregano

2 teaspoons paprika

2 teaspoons ground cumin

2 teaspoons sugar

½ teaspoon salt

¼ teaspoon red pepper flakes

¾ cup crumbled feta cheese

6 eggs

Chopped fresh cilantro (optional)

Black pepper (optional)

Toasted baguette slices (optional)

1 Spray inside of **CROCK-POT®** slow cooker with nonstick cooking spray. Combine oil, onion, bell pepper, garlic, tomatoes, paprika, cumin, sugar, salt and red pepper flakes in **CROCK-POT®** slow cooker. Cover; cook on HIGH 3 hours.

2 Stir in feta cheese; break eggs, one at a time, onto top of tomato mixture, leaving a little space between each. Cover; cook on HIGH 15 to 18 minutes or until the egg whites are set but yolks are still creamy. Scoop eggs and sauce evenly onto each serving dish. Garnish with cilantro and black pepper. Serve with baguette slices, if desired.

Curried Potatoes, Cauliflower and Peas

MAKES 6 SERVINGS

1 tablespoon vegetable oil

1 large yellow onion, chopped

2 tablespoons peeled and minced fresh ginger

2 cloves garlic, chopped

2 pounds red potatoes, cut into ½-inch-thick rounds

1 teaspoon garam masala*

1 teaspoon salt

1 small head cauliflower (about 1¼ pounds), trimmed and broken into florets

1 cup vegetable broth

2 plum tomatoes, seeded and chopped

1 cup frozen peas, thawed

Hot cooked basmati or long grain rice (optional)

*Garam masala is an Indian spice blend available in the spice aisle of many supermarkets. If garam masala is unavailable, substitute ½ teaspoon ground cumin and ½ teaspoon ground coriander seeds.

1 Heat oil in large skillet over medium heat. Add onion, ginger and garlic; cook and stir 3 to 5 minutes or until onion is tender. Remove from heat.

2 Place potatoes in **CROCK-POT**® slow cooker. Mix garam masala and salt in small bowl. Sprinkle half of spice mixture over potatoes. Top with onion mixture, then cauliflower. Sprinkle remaining spice mixture over cauliflower. Pour in broth. Cover; cook on HIGH 3½ hours.

3 Stir in tomatoes and peas. Cover; cook on HIGH 30 minutes or until potatoes are tender. Serve over rice, if desired.

CHICKEN & TURKEY

White Chicken Chili

MAKES 6 TO 8 SERVINGS

8 ounces dried navy beans, rinsed and sorted

1 tablespoon vegetable oil

2 pounds boneless, skinless chicken breasts (about 4)

2 onions, chopped

1 tablespoon minced garlic

2 teaspoons ground cumin

2 teaspoons salt

1 teaspoon dried oregano

¼ teaspoon black pepper

¼ teaspoon ground red pepper (optional)

4 cups chicken broth

1 can (4 ounces) fire-roasted diced mild green chiles, rinsed and drained

¼ cup chopped fresh cilantro

1 Place beans on bottom of **CROCK-POT**® slow cooker. Heat oil in large skillet over medium-high heat. Add chicken; cook 8 minutes or until browned on all sides. Remove to **CROCK-POT**® slow cooker.

2 Heat same skillet over medium heat. Add onions; cook 6 minutes or until softened and lightly browned. Add garlic, cumin, salt, oregano, black pepper and ground red pepper, if desired; cook and stir 1 minute. Add broth and chiles; bring to a simmer, stirring to scrape up any brown bits from bottom of skillet. Remove onion mixture to **CROCK-POT**® slow cooker.

3 Cover; cook on LOW 5 hours. Remove chicken to large cutting board; shred with two forks. Return chicken to **CROCK-POT**® slow cooker. Stir in cilantro.

Chinese Chicken Stew

MAKES 6 SERVINGS

1 pound boneless, skinless chicken thighs, cut into 1-inch pieces

1 teaspoon Chinese five-spice powder*

½ to ¾ teaspoon red pepper flakes

1 tablespoon peanut or vegetable oil

1 large onion, coarsely chopped

2 cloves garlic, minced

1 package (8 ounces) mushrooms, sliced

1 can (about 14 ounces) chicken broth, divided

1 tablespoon cornstarch

1 large red bell pepper, cut into ¾-inch pieces

2 tablespoons soy sauce

2 large green onions, cut into ½-inch pieces

1 tablespoon sesame oil

3 cups hot cooked rice (optional)

¼ cup coarsely chopped fresh cilantro (optional)

*Chinese five-spice powder is a blend of cinnamon, cloves, fennel seed, anise and Szechuan peppercorns. It is available in most supermarkets and Asian grocery stores.

1 Toss chicken with five-spice powder and red pepper flakes in large bowl. Heat peanut oil in large skillet. Add chicken and onion; cook and stir about 5 minutes or until chicken is browned. Add mushrooms and garlic; cook and stir 5 minutes or until chicken is no longer pink.

2 Stir ¼ cup broth into cornstarch in small bowl until smooth; set aside. Place chicken mixture, remaining broth, bell pepper and soy sauce in **CROCK-POT®** slow cooker. Cover; cook on LOW 3½ hours or until peppers are tender.

3 Whisk cornstarch mixture, green onions and sesame oil into **CROCK-POT®** slow cooker. Cover; cook on LOW 30 to 45 minutes or until thickened. Ladle into soup bowls. Scoop ½ cup rice into each bowl. Sprinkle with cilantro.

Turkey Stroganoff

MAKES 4 SERVINGS

Nonstick cooking spray

4 cups sliced mushrooms

2 stalks celery, thinly sliced

½ small onion, minced

1 cup chicken broth

½ teaspoon dried thyme

¼ teaspoon black pepper

2 turkey tenderloins, turkey breasts or boneless, skinless chicken thighs (about 10 ounces each), cut into 1-inch pieces

½ cup sour cream

1 tablespoon plus 1 teaspoon all-purpose flour

¼ teaspoon salt (optional)

1⅓ cups hot cooked wide egg noodles

1 Spray large skillet with cooking spray; heat over medium heat. Add mushrooms, celery and onion; cook and stir 5 minutes or until mushrooms and onion are tender. Spoon into **CROCK-POT®** slow cooker. Stir broth, thyme and pepper into **CROCK-POT®** slow cooker. Stir in turkey. Cover; cook on LOW 5 to 6 hours.

2 Stir sour cream into flour in small bowl. Spoon 2 tablespoons liquid from **CROCK-POT®** slow cooker into sour cream mixture; stir well. Whisk sour cream mixture into **CROCK-POT®** slow cooker. Cover; cook on LOW 10 minutes.

3 Season with salt, if desired. Spoon noodles onto each plate to serve. Top with turkey mixture.

Chicken Cacciatore

MAKES 6 SERVINGS

4 teaspoons olive oil

3 pounds boneless, skinless chicken breasts

½ teaspoon salt

¼ teaspoon black pepper

½ medium red bell pepper, sliced

½ medium green bell pepper, sliced

½ medium yellow bell pepper, sliced

1 cup onion, sliced

14 grape tomatoes

1½ cups water

¼ cup all-purpose flour

2 teaspoons garlic powder

1 teaspoon ground cumin

1 teaspoon dried oregano

1 teaspoon paprika

⅛ teaspoon ground red pepper

Hot cooked noodles or rice (optional)

1 Heat 2 teaspoons oil in large skillet over medium-high heat. Sprinkle chicken with salt and black pepper. Add half of chicken to skillet; cook 4 minutes per side or until browned. Remove to large plate. Repeat with remaining 2 teaspoons oil and chicken.

2 Add bell peppers, onion and grape tomatoes to **CROCK-POT**® slow cooker. Combine water, flour, garlic powder, cumin, oregano, paprika and ground red pepper in medium bowl; mix well. Add to **CROCK-POT**® slow cooker. Top with chicken. Cover; cook on LOW 8 to 9 hours or on HIGH 4 to 4½ hours. Serve with noodles, if desired.

Greek Chicken and Orzo

MAKES 4 SERVINGS

2 **medium green bell peppers, cut into thin strips**

1 **cup chopped onion**

2 **teaspoons extra virgin olive oil**

8 **chicken thighs, rinsed and patted dry**

1 **tablespoon dried oregano**

½ **teaspoon dried rosemary**

½ **teaspoon garlic powder**

¾ **teaspoon salt, divided**

½ **teaspoon black pepper, divided**

8 **ounces uncooked orzo pasta**

Juice and grated peel of 1 medium lemon

½ **cup water**

2 **ounces crumbled feta cheese (optional)**

Chopped fresh Italian parsley (optional)

1 Coat inside of **CROCK-POT®** slow cooker with nonstick cooking spray. Add bell peppers and onion.

2 Heat oil in large skillet over medium-high heat. Brown chicken on both sides. Remove to **CROCK-POT®** slow cooker, overlapping slightly if necessary. Sprinkle chicken with oregano, rosemary, garlic powder, ¼ teaspoon salt and ¼ teaspoon black pepper. Cover; cook on LOW 5 to 6 hours or on HIGH 3 to 4 hours or until chicken is tender.

3 Remove chicken to plate. Stir orzo, lemon juice, lemon peel, water, and remaining ½ teaspoon salt and ¼ teaspoon black pepper into **CROCK-POT®** slow cooker. Top with chicken. Cover; cook on HIGH 30 minutes or until pasta is tender. Garnish with feta cheese and parsley.

Tip: Browning skin-on chicken not only adds flavor and color, but also prevents the skin from shrinking and curling during the long, slow cooking process.

Chicken Orzo Soup

MAKES 8 SERVINGS

1 tablespoon vegetable oil

1 onion, diced

1 fennel bulb, quartered, cored, thinly sliced, tops removed and fronds reserved for garnish

2 teaspoons minced garlic

8 cups chicken broth

2 boneless, skinless chicken breasts (8 ounces *each*)

2 carrots, peeled and thinly sliced for topping

2 sprigs fresh thyme

1 whole bay leaf

½ cup uncooked orzo

1 Heat oil in large skillet over medium heat. Add onion and fennel; cook 8 minutes or until tender. Add garlic; cook and stir 1 minute. Remove to **CROCK-POT®** slow cooker. Add broth, chicken, carrots, thyme and bay leaf. Cover; cook on HIGH 2 to 3 hours.

2 Remove chicken to large cutting board; shred with two forks. Add orzo to **CROCK-POT®** slow cooker. Cover; cook on HIGH 30 minutes. Stir shredded chicken back into **CROCK-POT®** slow cooker. Remove and discard thyme sprigs and bay leaf. Garnish each serving with fennel fronds.

Chicken Congee

MAKES 6 SERVINGS

6 **cups water**

4 **cups chicken broth**

4 **chicken drumsticks**

1 **cup uncooked white jasmine rice, rinsed and drained**

1 **(1-inch) piece fresh ginger, sliced into 4 pieces**

2 **teaspoons kosher salt**

¼ **teaspoon ground white pepper**

Optional toppings: soy sauce, sesame oil, thinly sliced green onions, fried shallots, fried garlic slices, salted roasted peanuts and/or pickled vegetables

1 Add water, broth, chicken, rice, ginger, salt and pepper to **CHICKEN** slow cooker. Cover; cook on LOW 8 hours or on HIGH 4 hours or until rice has completely broken down and mixture is thickened.

2 Remove and discard ginger. Remove chicken to large cutting board. Discard skin and bones. Shred chicken using two forks. Stir chicken back into **CROCK-POT**® slow cooker. Ladle congee into serving bowls; top with desired toppings.

Country Chicken and Vegetables with Creamy Herb Sauce

MAKES 4 SERVINGS

1 pound new potatoes, cut into ½-inch wedges

1 medium onion, cut into 8 wedges

½ cup coarsely chopped celery

4 bone-in chicken drumsticks, skinned

4 bone-in chicken thighs, skinned

1 can (10¾ ounces) cream of chicken soup

1 packet (1 ounce) ranch-style dressing mix

½ teaspoon dried thyme

¼ teaspoon black pepper

½ cup whipping cream

Salt

¼ cup finely chopped green onions (green and white parts)

1 Coat inside of **CROCK-POT**® slow cooker with nonstick cooking spray. Arrange potatoes, onion and celery in bottom. Add chicken. Combine soup, dressing mix, thyme and pepper in small bowl. Spoon mixture evenly over chicken and vegetables. Cover; cook on HIGH 3½ hours.

2 Remove chicken to shallow serving bowl with slotted spoon. Add cream and salt to cooking liquid; stir to blend. Pour sauce over chicken. Garnish with green onions.

Note: To skin chicken easily, grasp skin with paper towel and pull away. Repeat with fresh paper towel for each piece of chicken, discarding skins and towels.

Spanish Chicken with Rice

MAKES 6 SERVINGS

- **2 tablespoons olive oil**
- **11 ounces cooked linguiça or kielbasa sausage, sliced into ½-inch rounds**
- **6 boneless, skinless chicken thighs (about 1 pound)**
- **1 onion, chopped**
- **5 cloves garlic, minced**
- **2 cups uncooked converted long grain rice**
- **½ cup diced carrots**
- **1 red bell pepper, chopped**
- **½ teaspoon salt**
- **¼ teaspoon black pepper**
- **¼ teaspoon saffron threads (optional)**
- **3½ cups hot chicken broth**
- **½ cup peas**

1 Heat oil in medium skillet over medium heat. Add sausage; cook and stir until browned. Remove to **CROCK-POT®** slow cooker using slotted spoon.

2 Add chicken to skillet; brown on all sides. Remove to **CROCK-POT®** slow cooker. Add onion to skillet; cook and stir 5 minutes or until soft. Stir in garlic; cook 30 seconds. Remove to **CROCK-POT®** slow cooker.

3 Add rice, carrots, bell pepper, salt, black pepper and saffron, if desired, to **CROCK-POT®** slow cooker. Pour broth over mixture. Cover; cook on HIGH 3½ to 4 hours.

4 Stir in peas. Cover; cook on HIGH 15 minutes or until heated through.

Hearty Cassoulet

MAKES 6 SERVINGS

- **1 tablespoon olive oil**
- **1 onion, finely chopped**
- **4 boneless, skinless chicken thighs, chopped**
- **¼ pound smoked turkey sausage, finely chopped**
- **3 cloves garlic, minced**
- **1 teaspoon dried thyme**
- **½ teaspoon black pepper**
- **¼ cup tomato paste**
- **2 tablespoons water**
- **3 cans (about 15 ounces each) cannellini beans, rinsed and drained**
- **½ cup plain dry bread crumbs**
- **3 tablespoons minced fresh Italian parsley**

1 Heat oil in large skillet over medium heat. Add onion; cook and stir 5 minutes or until tender. Add chicken, sausage, garlic, thyme and pepper; cook and stir 5 minutes or until chicken and sausage are browned.

2 Remove from heat; stir in tomato paste and water until blended. Remove to **CROCK-POT**® slow cooker. Stir in beans. Cover; cook on LOW 4 to 4½ hours.

3 Combine bread crumbs and parsley in small bowl; toss to blend. Sprinkle over top of cassoulet just before serving.

Tip: When preparing ingredients for the **CROCK-POT**® slow cooker, cut into uniform pieces so everything will cook evenly.

Thai-Style Chicken Pumpkin Soup

MAKES 4 TO 6 SERVINGS

1 tablespoon olive oil

6 boneless, skinless chicken breasts, cut into 1-inch cubes

1 white onion, thinly sliced

3 cloves garlic, minced

1 tablespoon minced fresh ginger

½ to ¾ teaspoon red pepper flakes

2 stalks celery, diced

2 carrots, diced

1 can (15 ounces) solid-pack pumpkin*

½ cup creamy peanut butter

4 cups chicken broth

½ cup mango nectar

½ cup lime juice

3 tablespoons rice vinegar

½ cup minced fresh cilantro, divided

½ cup whipping cream

1 tablespoon cornstarch

2 to 4 cups hot cooked rice

3 green onions, minced

½ cup roasted unsalted peanuts, coarsely chopped

Lime wedges (optional)

*Do not use pumpkin pie filling.

1 Heat oil in large skillet over medium heat. Add chicken; cook and stir 3 minutes. Add onion, garlic, ginger and red pepper flakes; cook 2 minutes or until fragrant. Remove chicken mixture to **CROCK-POT®** slow cooker.

2 Stir in celery, carrots, pumpkin, peanut butter, broth, mango nectar and lime juice. Cover; cook on LOW 8 hours or on HIGH 4 hours.

3 Stir in rice vinegar and ¼ cup cilantro. Stir cream into cornstarch in small bowl; whisk into **CROCK-POT®** slow cooker. Simmer, uncovered, on HIGH 10 minutes or until soup is thickened.

4 To serve, put rice in soup bowls. Ladle soup around rice. Sprinkle with remaining ¼ cup cilantro, green onions and peanuts. Squeeze fresh lime juice over soup, if desired.

Pomegranate Chicken

MAKES 6 SERVINGS

4 cups pomegranate juice

2 cups walnuts, toasted*

1 tablespoon vegetable oil

1 large onion, finely diced

3 pounds chicken wings

2 tablespoons sugar

¼ teaspoon ground cinnamon

¼ teaspoon kosher salt

¼ teaspoon black pepper

Hot cooked Israeli couscous (optional)

Pomegranate seeds (optional)

Chopped fresh cilantro (optional)

*To toast walnuts, spread in single layer in small heavy skillet. Cook and stir 1 to 2 minutes over medium heat until nuts are lightly browned, stirring frequently. Remove from skillet immediately.

1 Pour pomegranate juice into small saucepan; bring to a boil over high heat. Boil 18 to 20 minutes or until juice is reduced to 2 cups.

2 Meanwhile, place walnuts in food processor; pulse until finely ground. Remove to **CROCK-POT**® slow cooker.

3 Heat oil in large skillet over medium-high heat. Add onion; cook 6 minutes or until translucent. Add wings, onion mixture, pomegranate juice, sugar, cinnamon, salt and pepper to **CROCK-POT**® slow cooker.

4 Cover; cook on HIGH 3 to 4 hours. Serve over couscous, if desired. Garnish with pomegranate seeds and cilantro.

Spanish Paella with Chicken and Sausage

MAKES 4 SERVINGS

1 tablespoon olive oil

4 chicken thighs (about 2 pounds total)

1 medium onion, chopped

4 cups chicken broth

1 pound hot smoked sausage, sliced into rounds

1 can (about 14 ounces) stewed tomatoes, undrained

1 cup uncooked Arborio rice

1 clove garlic, minced

1 pinch saffron threads (optional)

½ cup frozen peas, thawed

1 Heat oil in large skillet over medium-high heat. Add chicken in batches; cook 5 to 7 minutes or until browned on all sides. Remove chicken to **CROCK-POT®** slow cooker as it browns.

2 Add onion to same skillet; cook 6 to 8 minutes or until translucent. Stir broth, sausage, tomatoes, rice and garlic into skillet. Stir in saffron, if desired. Pour over chicken in **CROCK-POT®** slow cooker. Cover; cook on LOW 6 to 8 hours or on HIGH 3 to 4 hours or until chicken is fully cooked and rice is tender.

3 Remove chicken pieces to large plate; fluff rice with fork. Stir peas into rice. Spoon rice into bowls; top with chicken.

Chipotle Chicken Stew

MAKES 6 SERVINGS

1 pound boneless, skinless chicken thighs, cut into cubes

1 can (about 15 ounces) navy beans, rinsed and drained

1 can (about 15 ounces) black beans, rinsed and drained

1 can (about 14 ounces) crushed tomatoes, undrained

1½ cups chicken broth

½ cup orange juice

1 medium onion, diced

1 canned chipotle pepper in adobo sauce, minced

1 teaspoon salt

1 teaspoon ground cumin

1 whole bay leaf

Sprigs fresh cilantro (optional)

1 Combine chicken, beans, tomatoes, broth, orange juice, onion, chipotle pepper, salt, cumin and bay leaf in **CROCK-POT®** slow cooker; stir to blend.

2 Cover; cook on LOW 7 to 8 hours or on HIGH 3½ to 4 hours. Remove and discard bay leaf. Garnish with cilantro.

Chicken Scaloppine in Alfredo Sauce

MAKES 6 SERVINGS

2 tablespoons all-purpose flour

¼ **teaspoon salt**

¼ **teaspoon black pepper**

6 boneless, skinless chicken tenderloins (about 1 pound), cut lengthwise in half

1 tablespoon butter

1 tablespoon olive oil

1 cup Alfredo pasta sauce

1 package (12 ounces) uncooked spinach noodles

1 Place flour, salt and pepper in large bowl; stir to combine. Add chicken; toss to coat. Heat butter and oil in large skillet over medium-high heat. Add chicken; cook 3 minutes per side or until browned. Remove chicken in single layer to **CROCK-POT®** slow cooker.

2 Add Alfredo pasta sauce to **CROCK-POT®** slow cooker. Cover; cook on LOW 1 to 1½ hours.

3 Meanwhile, cook noodles according to package directions. Drain; place in large shallow bowl. Spoon chicken and sauce over noodles.

ON THE SIDE

Chunky Ranch Potatoes

MAKES 8 SERVINGS

3 **pounds unpeeled red potatoes, quartered**

1 **cup water**

½ **cup prepared ranch dressing**

½ **cup grated Parmesan or Cheddar cheese**

¼ **cup minced fresh chives**

Place potatoes in **CROCK-POT®** slow cooker. Add water. Cover; cook on LOW 7 to 9 hours or on HIGH 4 to 6 hours. Stir in ranch dressing, cheese and chives.

Cheesy Polenta

MAKES 6 SERVINGS

6 cups vegetable broth

1½ cups uncooked medium-grind instant polenta

½ cup grated Parmesan cheese, plus additional for serving

4 tablespoons (½ stick) unsalted butter, cubed

Fried sage leaves (optional)

1 Coat inside of **CROCK-POT**® slow cooker with nonstick cooking spray. Heat broth in large saucepan over high heat. Remove to **CROCK-POT**® slow cooker; whisk in polenta.

2 Cover; cook on LOW 2 to 2½ hours or until polenta is tender and creamy. Stir in ½ cup cheese and butter. Serve with additional cheese. Garnish with sage.

Tip: Spread any leftover polenta in a baking dish and refrigerate until cold. Cut cold polenta into sticks or slices. You can then fry or grill the polenta until lightly browned.

Mashed Root Vegetables

MAKES 6 SERVINGS

1 pound baking potatoes, peeled and cut into 1-inch pieces

1 pound turnips, peeled and cut into 1-inch pieces

12 ounces sweet potatoes, peeled and cut into 1-inch pieces

8 ounces parsnips, peeled and cut into ½-inch pieces

5 tablespoons butter

¼ cup water

2 teaspoons salt

¼ teaspoon black pepper

1 cup milk

1 Coat inside of **CROCK-POT**® slow cooker with nonstick cooking spray. Add baking potatoes, turnips, sweet potatoes, parsnips, butter, water, salt and pepper; stir to blend. Cover; cook on HIGH 3 to 4 hours.

2 Mash mixture with potato masher until smooth. Stir in milk. Cover; cook on HIGH 15 minutes.

Frijoles Borrachos

MAKES 8 SERVINGS

- **6 slices bacon, chopped**
- **1 medium yellow onion, chopped**
- **1 tablespoon minced garlic**
- **3 jalapeño peppers, seeded and finely diced***
- **1 tablespoon dried oregano**
- **1 can (12 ounces) beer**
- **6 cups water**

- **1 pound dried pinto beans, rinsed and sorted**
- **1 can (about 14 ounces) diced tomatoes**
- **1 tablespoon kosher salt**
- **¼ cup chopped fresh cilantro**

*Jalapeño peppers can sting and irritate the skin, so wear rubber gloves when handling peppers and do not touch your eyes.

1 Heat large skillet over medium heat. Add bacon; cook and stir 5 minutes or until crisp. Remove to **CROCK-POT**® slow cooker using slotted spoon. Discard all but 3 tablespoons of drippings.

2 Return same skillet to medium heat. Add onion; cook 6 minutes or until softened and lightly browned. Add garlic, jalapeño peppers and oregano; cook 30 seconds or until fragrant. Increase heat to medium-high. Add beer; bring to a simmer. Cook 2 minutes, stirring and scraping any brown bits from bottom of skillet. Remove mixture to **CROCK-POT**® slow cooker.

3 Add water, beans, tomatoes and salt to **CROCK-POT**® slow cooker. Cover; cook on LOW 7 hours or on HIGH 3 to 4 hours or until beans are tender. Mash beans slightly until broth is thickened and creamy. Top with cilantro.

Lemon and Tangerine Glazed Carrots

MAKES 10 TO 12 SERVINGS

6	**cups sliced carrots**
1½	**cups apple juice**
6	**tablespoons butter**
¼	**cup packed brown sugar**
2	**tablespoons grated lemon peel**
2	**tablespoons grated tangerine peel**
½	**teaspoon salt**
	Chopped fresh Italian parsley (optional)

Combine carrots, apple juice, butter, brown sugar, lemon peel, tangerine peel and salt in **CROCK-POT®** slow cooker; stir to blend. Cover; cook on LOW 4 to 5 hours or on HIGH 1 to 3 hours. Garnish with parsley.

Cheesy Corn and Peppers

MAKES 8 SERVINGS

- 2 pounds frozen corn
- 2 poblano peppers, chopped
- 2 tablespoons butter, cubed
- 1 teaspoon salt
- ½ teaspoon ground cumin
- ¼ teaspoon black pepper
- 3 ounces cream cheese, cubed
- 1 cup (4 ounces) shredded sharp Cheddar cheese

1 Coat inside of **CROCK-POT**® slow cooker with nonstick cooking spray. Combine corn, poblano peppers, butter, salt, cumin and black pepper in **CROCK-POT**® slow cooker. Cover; cook on HIGH 2 hours.

2 Stir in cheeses. Cover; cook on HIGH 15 minutes or until cheeses are melted.

Artichoke and Tomato Paella

MAKES 8 SERVINGS

- **4 cups vegetable broth**
- **2 cups uncooked converted rice**
- **½ (10-ounce) package frozen chopped spinach, thawed and drained**
- **1 green bell pepper, chopped**
- **1 medium tomato, chopped**
- **1 medium yellow onion, chopped**

- **1 medium carrot, diced**
- **3 cloves garlic, minced**
- **1 tablespoon minced fresh Italian parsley**
- **½ teaspoon salt**
- **½ teaspoon black pepper**
- **1 can (13¾ ounces) artichoke hearts, quartered, rinsed and well drained**
- **½ cup frozen peas, thawed**

Combine broth, rice, spinach, bell pepper, tomato, onion, carrot, garlic, parsley, salt and black pepper in **CROCK-POT**® slow cooker; stir to blend. Cover; cook on LOW 4 hours or on HIGH 2 hours. Stir in artichoke hearts and peas. Cover; cook on HIGH 15 minutes.

Lemon-Mint Red Potatoes

MAKES 4 SERVINGS

2 **pounds new red potatoes**

3 **tablespoons extra virgin olive oil**

1 **teaspoon salt**

½ **teaspoon Greek seasoning or dried oregano**

¼ **teaspoon garlic powder**

¼ **teaspoon black pepper**

4 **tablespoons chopped fresh mint, divided**

2 **tablespoons butter**

2 **tablespoons lemon juice**

1 **teaspoon grated lemon peel**

1 Coat inside of **CROCK-POT®** slow cooker with nonstick cooking spray. Add potatoes and oil, stirring gently to coat. Sprinkle with salt, Greek seasoning, garlic powder and pepper. Cover; cook on LOW 7 hours or on HIGH 4 hours.

2 Stir in 2 tablespoons mint, butter, lemon juice and lemon peel until butter is completely melted. Cover; cook on HIGH 15 minutes. Sprinkle with remaining 2 tablespoons mint.

Tip: It's easy to prepare these potatoes ahead of time. Simply follow the recipe and then turn off the heat. Let it stand at room temperature for up to 2 hours. You may reheat or serve the potatoes at room temperature.

Lemon Cauliflower

MAKES 6 SERVINGS

1 tablespoon butter	**½ teaspoon grated lemon peel**
3 cloves garlic, minced	**6 cups (about 1½ pounds) cauliflower florets**
2 tablespoons lemon juice	
½ cup water	**¼ cup grated Parmesan cheese**
4 tablespoons chopped fresh Italian parsley, divided	**Lemon slices (optional)**

1 Heat butter in small saucepan over medium heat. Add garlic; cook and stir 2 to 3 minutes or until soft. Stir in lemon juice and water.

2 Combine garlic mixture, 1 tablespoon parsley, lemon peel and cauliflower in **CROCK-POT**® slow cooker; stir to blend. Cover; cook on LOW 4 hours.

3 Sprinkle with remaining 3 tablespoons parsley and cheese before serving. Garnish with lemon slices.

Asian Golden Barley with Cashews

MAKES 4 SERVINGS

2 tablespoons olive oil	**1 medium yellow onion, chopped**
1 cup hulled barley, sorted	**1 clove garlic, minced**
3 cups vegetable broth	**¼ teaspoon black pepper**
1 cup chopped celery	**Chopped cashew nuts**
1 medium green bell pepper, chopped	

1 Heat large skillet over medium heat. Add oil and barley; cook and stir 10 minutes or until barley is slightly browned. Remove to **CROCK-POT®** slow cooker.

2 Add broth, celery, bell pepper, onion, garlic and black pepper; stir to blend. Cover; cook on LOW 4 to 5 hours or on HIGH 2 to 3 hours or until liquid is absorbed. Top with cashews.

Swiss Cheese Scalloped Potatoes

MAKES 5 TO 6 SERVINGS

2	**pounds baking potatoes, peeled and thinly sliced**
½	**cup finely chopped yellow onion**
¼	**teaspoon salt**
¼	**teaspoon ground nutmeg**
2	**tablespoons butter, cut into small pieces**

½	**cup milk**
2	**tablespoons all-purpose flour**
¾	**cup (3 ounces) shredded Swiss cheese**
¼	**cup finely chopped green onions**

1 Layer half of potatoes, ¼ cup onion, ⅛ teaspoon salt, ⅛ teaspoon nutmeg and 1 tablespoon butter in **CROCK-POT®** slow cooker. Repeat layers. Cover; cook on LOW 7 hours or on HIGH 4 hours.

2 Remove potatoes with slotted spoon to serving dish; keep warm.

3 Stir milk into flour in small bowl until smooth; whisk into **CROCK-POT®** slow cooker. Stir in cheese. Cover; cook on HIGH 10 minutes or until slightly thickened. Stir. Pour cheese mixture over potatoes. Sprinkle with green onions.

White Beans and Tomatoes

MAKES 8 TO 10 SERVINGS

¼ **cup olive oil**

2 **medium onions, chopped**

1 **tablespoon minced garlic**

2 **cans (about 14 ounces each) cannellini beans, rinsed and drained**

1 **can (about 28 ounces) crushed tomatoes**

4 **cups water**

2 **teaspoons kosher salt**

4 **teaspoons dried oregano**

Black pepper (optional)

Sprigs fresh oregano (optional)

1 Heat oil in large skillet over medium heat. Add onions; cook 15 minutes or until tender and translucent, stirring occasionally. Add garlic; cook 1 minute.

2 Remove mixture to **CROCK-POT**® slow cooker. Add beans, tomatoes, water and salt. Cover; cook on LOW 8 hours or on HIGH 4 hours. Stir in dried oregano and pepper, if desired. Garnish with fresh oregano.

Colcannon

MAKES 8 SERVINGS

6 **tablespoons butter, cut into small pieces**

3 **pounds russet potatoes, peeled and cut into 1-inch pieces**

2 **medium leeks, white and light green parts only, thinly sliced**

½ **cup water**

2½ **teaspoons kosher salt**

¼ **teaspoon black pepper**

1 **cup milk**

½ **small head (about 1 pound) savoy cabbage, cored and thinly sliced**

4 **slices bacon, crisp-cooked and crumbled**

1 Sprinkle butter on bottom of **CROCK-POT**® slow cooker. Layer half of potatoes, leeks, remaining potatoes, water, salt and pepper. Cover; cook on HIGH 5 hours or until potatoes are tender, stirring halfway through cooking time.

2 Mash potatoes in **CROCK-POT**® slow cooker until smooth. Stir in milk and cabbage. Cover; cook on HIGH 30 to 40 minutes or until cabbage is crisp-tender. Stir bacon into potato mixture.

Red Cabbage and Apples

MAKES 6 SERVINGS

1 small head red cabbage, cored and thinly sliced

1 large apple, peeled and grated

¾ cup sugar

½ cup red wine vinegar

1 teaspoon ground cloves

Fresh apple slices (optional)

Combine cabbage, grated apple, sugar, vinegar and cloves in **CROCK-POT®** slow cooker; stir to blend. Cover; cook on HIGH 6 hours, stirring halfway through cooking time. Garnish with apple slices.

BBQ Baked Beans

MAKES 12 SERVINGS

3 cans (about 15 ounces *each*)
   white beans, drained

4 slices bacon, chopped

¾ cup prepared barbecue
   sauce

½ cup maple syrup

1½ teaspoons dry mustard

Coat inside of **CROCK-POT**® slow cooker with nonstick cooking spray. Add beans, bacon, barbecue sauce, syrup and mustard; stir to blend. Cover; cook on LOW 4 hours, stirring halfway through cooking time.

Coconut-Lime
Sweet Potatoes with Walnuts

MAKES 8 SERVINGS

2½ **pounds sweet potatoes, cut into 1-inch pieces**

8 **ounces shredded carrots**

¾ **cup shredded coconut, toasted and divided***

1 **tablespoon unsalted butter, melted**

3 **tablespoons sugar**

½ **teaspoon salt**

3 **tablespoons walnuts, toasted and coarsely chopped****

2 **teaspoons grated lime peel**

*To toast coconut, spread in single layer in heavy-bottomed skillet. Cook over medium heat 1 to 2 minutes until lightly browned, stirring frequently. Remove from skillet.

**To toast walnuts, spread in single layer in small skillet. Cook and stir over medium heat 1 to 2 minutes or until nuts are lightly browned.

1 Combine potatoes, carrots, ½ cup coconut, butter, sugar and salt in **CROCK-POT**® slow cooker. Cover; cook on LOW 5 to 6 hours. Remove to large bowl.

2 Mash potatoes with potato masher. Stir in walnuts and lime peel. Sprinkle with remaining ¼ cup coconut.

DELICIOUS DESSERTS

Cinnamon Roll-Topped Mixed Berry Cobbler

MAKES 8 SERVINGS

2 bags (12 ounces *each*) frozen mixed berries, thawed

1 cup sugar

¼ cup quick-cooking tapioca

¼ cup water

2 teaspoons vanilla

1 package (about 12 ounces) refrigerated cinnamon rolls with icing

Combine berries, sugar, tapioca, water and vanilla in **CROCK-POT®** slow cooker; top with cinnamon rolls. Cover; cook on LOW 4 to 5 hours. Serve warm; drizzled with icing.

Note: This recipe was designed to work best in a 4-quart **CROCK-POT®** slow cooker. Double the ingredients for larger **CROCK-POT®** slow cookers, but always place cinnamon rolls in a single layer.

Apple-Pecan Bread Pudding

MAKES 8 SERVINGS

8   cups bread cubes

3   cups Granny Smith apples,
    cubed

1   cup chopped pecans

8   eggs

1   can (12 ounces) evaporated
    milk

1   cup packed brown sugar

½   cup apple cider or apple
    juice

2   teaspoons ground cinnamon

1   teaspoon ground nutmeg

1   teaspoon vanilla

½   teaspoon salt

½   teaspoon ground allspice
    Ice cream (optional)
    Caramel topping (optional)

1 Coat inside of **CROCK-POT**® slow cooker with nonstick cooking spray.
Add bread cubes, apples and pecans.

2 Combine eggs, evaporated milk, brown sugar, apple cider, cinnamon,
nutmeg, vanilla, salt and allspice in large bowl; whisk to blend. Pour egg
mixture into **CROCK-POT**® slow cooker. Cover; cook on LOW 3 hours. Serve
with ice cream topped with caramel sauce, if desired.

Pumpkin Bread Pudding

MAKES 8 SERVINGS

2 cups whole milk

½ cup (1 stick) plus 2 tablespoons butter, divided

1 cup packed brown sugar, divided

1 cup canned solid-pack pumpkin

3 eggs

1 tablespoon ground cinnamon

2 teaspoons vanilla

½ teaspoon ground nutmeg

¼ teaspoon salt

16 slices cinnamon raisin bread, torn into small pieces (8 cups total)

½ cup whipping cream

2 tablespoons bourbon (optional)

1 Coat inside of **CROCK-POT**® slow cooker with nonstick cooking spray. Combine milk and 2 tablespoons butter in medium microwavable bowl. Microwave on HIGH 2½ to 3 minutes or until very warm.

2 Whisk ½ cup brown sugar, pumpkin, eggs, cinnamon, vanilla, nutmeg and salt in large bowl until well blended. Whisk in milk mixture until blended. Add bread pieces; toss to coat. Remove bread mixture to **CROCK-POT**® slow cooker.

3 Cover; cook on HIGH 2 hours or until knife inserted into center comes out clean. Turn off heat. Uncover; let stand 15 minutes.

4 Combine remaining ½ cup butter, remaining ½ cup brown sugar and cream in small saucepan; bring to a boil over high heat, stirring frequently. Remove from heat. Stir in bourbon, if desired. Spoon bread pudding into individual bowls; top with sauce.

Apple Crumble Pot

MAKES 6 TO 8 SERVINGS

4 **Granny Smith apples (about 2 pounds), cored and each cut into 8 wedges**

1 **cup packed dark brown sugar, divided**

½ **cup dried cranberries**

1 **cup plus 2 tablespoons biscuit baking mix, divided**

2 **tablespoons butter, cubed**

1½ **teaspoons ground cinnamon, plus additional for topping**

1 **teaspoon vanilla**

¼ **teaspoon ground allspice**

½ **cup rolled oats**

3 **tablespoons cold butter, cubed**

½ **cup chopped pecans**

Whipped cream (optional)

1 Coat inside of **CROCK-POT®** slow cooker with nonstick cooking spray. Combine apples, ⅔ cup brown sugar, cranberries, 2 tablespoons baking mix, 2 tablespoons butter, 1½ teaspoons cinnamon, vanilla and allspice in **CROCK-POT®** slow cooker; toss gently to coat.

2 Combine remaining 1 cup baking mix, oats and remaining ⅓ cup brown sugar in large bowl. Cut in 3 tablespoons cold butter with pastry blender or two knives until mixture resembles coarse crumbs. Sprinkle evenly over filling in **CROCK-POT®** slow cooker. Top with pecans. Cover; cook on HIGH 2¼ hours or until apples are tender. *Do not overcook.*

3 Turn off heat. Let stand, uncovered, 15 to 30 minutes before serving. Top with whipped cream sprinkled with additional cinnamon, if desired.

Luscious Pecan Bread Pudding

MAKES 6 SERVINGS

3 cups day-old **French bread cubes**

3 tablespoons chopped **pecans, toasted***

2¼ cups **milk**

2 **eggs, beaten**

½ cup **sugar**

1 teaspoon **vanilla**

¾ **teaspoon ground cinnamon, divided**

¾ cup **cranberry juice cocktail**

1½ cups **frozen pitted tart cherries**

2 tablespoons **sugar**

*To toast pecans, spread in single layer in heavy skillet. Cook over medium heat 1 to 2 minutes or until nuts are lightly browned, stirring frequently.

1 Prepare foil handles by tearing off three (18×2-inch) strips of heavy foil or use regular foil folded to double thickness. Crisscross foil strips in spoke design and place in **CROCK-POT**® slow cooker. Toss bread cubes and pecans in soufflé dish that fits inside of **CROCK-POT**® slow cooker.

2 Combine milk, eggs, sugar, vanilla and ½ teaspoon cinnamon in large bowl; pour over bread mixture in soufflé dish. Cover tightly with foil. Place soufflé dish in **CROCK-POT**® slow cooker. Pour hot water into **CROCK-POT**® slow cooker to about 1½ inches from top of soufflé dish. Cover; cook on LOW 2 to 3 hours.

3 Meanwhile, combine cranberry juice and remaining ¼ teaspoon cinnamon in small saucepan; stir in cherries. Bring to a boil over medium heat; cook 5 minutes. Remove from heat. Stir in sugar.

4 Lift soufflé dish from **CROCK-POT**® slow cooker using foil handles. Serve bread pudding with cherry sauce.

Peach Cobbler

MAKES 4 TO 6 SERVINGS

2   **packages (16 ounces** *each***)
    frozen peaches, thawed
    and drained**

½   **cup plus 1 tablespoon sugar,
    divided**

2   **teaspoons ground cinnamon,
    divided**

½   **teaspoon ground nutmeg**

¾   **cup all-purpose flour**

6   **tablespoons butter, cubed**
    Whipped cream (optional)

1 Coat inside of **CROCK-POT**® slow cooker with nonstick cooking spray.
Combine peaches, ½ cup sugar, 1½ teaspoons cinnamon and nutmeg in
CROCK-POT® slow cooker; stir to blend.

2 Combine flour, remaining 1 tablespoon sugar and remaining ½ teaspoon
cinnamon in small bowl. Cut in butter with pastry blender or two knives
until mixture resembles coarse crumbs. Sprinkle over peach mixture. Cover;
cook on HIGH 2 hours. Serve with whipped cream, if desired.

Brioche and Amber Rum Custard

MAKES 4 TO 6 SERVINGS

2 tablespoons unsalted butter, melted

3½ cups whipping cream

4 eggs

½ cup packed dark brown sugar

⅓ cup amber or light rum

2 teaspoons vanilla

1 loaf (20 to 22 ounces) brioche bread, torn into small pieces or 5 large brioche, cut into thirds*

½ cup coarsely chopped pecans

Caramel or butterscotch topping (optional)

*If desired, trim and discard heels.

1 Butter inside of **CROCK-POT®** slow cooker with melted butter. Combine cream, eggs, brown sugar, rum and vanilla in large bowl; stir well.

2 Mound one fourth of brioche pieces in bottom of **CROCK-POT®** slow cooker. Ladle one fourth of cream mixture over brioche. Sprinkle with one third of pecans. Repeat layers with remaining brioche, cream mixture and pecans until all ingredients are used.

3 Cover; cook on LOW 3 to 3½ hours or on HIGH 1½ to 2 hours or until custard is set and toothpick inserted into center comes out clean.

4 Drizzle with caramel or butterscotch topping, if desired. Serve warm.

Spiced Apple and Cranberry Compote

MAKES 6 SERVINGS

2½ cups cranberry juice cocktail

1 package (6 ounces) dried apples

½ cup (2 ounces) dried cranberries

½ cup **Rhine wine or apple juice**

½ cup honey

2 cinnamon sticks, broken in half

Frozen ice cream or yogurt (optional)

Combine cranberry juice, apples, cranberries, wine, honey and cinnamon stick halves in **CROCK-POT®** slow cooker; stir to blend. Cover; cook on LOW 4 to 5 hours or until liquid is absorbed and fruit is tender. Remove and discard cinnamon stick halves. Serve with ice cream, if desired.

Cherry Delight

MAKES 8 TO 10 SERVINGS

1 **can (21 ounces) cherry pie**
   filling

1 **package (about 18 ounces)**
   yellow cake mix

½ **cup (1 stick) butter, melted**

⅓ **cup chopped walnuts**

Place pie filling in **CROCK-POT®** slow cooker. Combine cake mix and butter in medium bowl; stir to blend. Spread evenly over pie filling. Sprinkle with walnuts. Cover; cook on LOW 3 to 4 hours or on HIGH 1½ to 2 hours.

Pumpkin-Cranberry Custard

MAKES 4 TO 6 SERVINGS

1 can (30 ounces) pumpkin
  pie filling
1 can (12 ounces) evaporated
  milk

1 cup dried cranberries
4 eggs, beaten
1 cup whole gingersnap
  cookies (optional)

Combine pumpkin, evaporated milk, cranberries and eggs in **CROCK-POT**®
slow cooker; stir to blend. Cover; cook on HIGH 4 to 4½ hours. Serve with
gingersnaps, if desired.

Poached Autumn Fruits with Vanilla-Citrus Broth

MAKES 4 TO 6 SERVINGS

2 **Granny Smith apples, peeled, cored and halved (reserve cores)**

2 **Bartlett pears, peeled, cored and halved (reserve cores)**

1 **orange, peeled and halved**

½ **cup dried cranberries, plus additional for topping**

⅓ **cup sugar**

5 **tablespoons honey**

1 **vanilla bean, split and seeded (reserve seeds)**

1 **whole cinnamon stick**

Vanilla ice cream (optional)

1 Place apple and pear cores in **CROCK-POT®** slow cooker. Squeeze juice from orange halves into **CROCK-POT®** slow cooker. Add orange halves, ½ cup cranberries, sugar, honey, vanilla bean and seeds and cinnamon stick. Add apples and pears. Pour in enough water to cover fruit. Stir gently to combine. Cover; cook on HIGH 2 hours or until fruit is tender.

2 Remove apple and pear halves; set aside. Strain cooking liquid into large saucepan. (Discard solids.) Simmer gently over low heat until liquid is reduced by half and thickened.

3 Dice apple and pear halves. Add to saucepan to rewarm fruit. To serve, spoon fruit with sauce into bowls. Top with additional cranberries and vanilla ice cream, if desired.

Steamed Southern Sweet Potato Custard

MAKES 4 SERVINGS

- **1 can (16 ounces) cut sweet potatoes, drained**
- **1 can (12 ounces) evaporated milk, divided**
- **½ cup packed brown sugar**
- **2 eggs, lightly beaten**
- **1 teaspoon ground cinnamon**
- **½ teaspoon ground ginger**
- **¼ teaspoon salt**
- **Whipped cream (optional)**
- **Ground nutmeg (optional)**

1 Place potatoes and ¼ cup evaporated milk in food processor or blender; process until smooth. Add remaining evaporated milk, brown sugar, eggs, cinnamon, ginger and salt; process until well blended. Pour into ungreased 1-quart soufflé dish; cover tightly with foil. Crumple large sheet (15×12 inches) of foil; place in bottom of **CROCK-POT**® slow cooker. Pour 2 cups water over foil.

2 Prepare foil handles by tearing off three 18×2-inch strips of heavy-duty foil or use regular foil folded to double thickness. Crisscross strips in spoke design and place in **CROCK-POT**® slow cooker. Place soufflé dish in **CROCK-POT**® slow cooker. Cover; cook on HIGH 2½ to 3 hours or until skewer inserted into center comes out clean.

3 Use foil handles to remove dish to wire rack. Uncover; let stand 30 minutes. Garnish with whipped cream and nutmeg.

Citrus Chinese Dates with Toasted Hazelnuts

MAKES 4 SERVINGS

2 cups pitted dates

⅔ cup boiling water

½ cup sugar

Strips of peel from 1 lemon (yellow part only)

¼ cup hazelnuts, shelled and toasted*

Whipped cream (optional)

*To toast hazelnuts, spread in single layer in heavy skillet. Cook and stir over medium heat 1 to 2 minutes or until nuts are lightly browned.

1 Place dates in medium bowl; cover with water. Soak overnight to rehydrate. Drain. Remove dates to **CROCK-POT®** slow cooker.

2 Add ⅔ cup boiling water, sugar and lemon peel to **CROCK-POT®** slow cooker. Cover; cook on HIGH 3 hours.

3 Remove and discard peel. Place dates in serving dishes. Sprinkle with hazelnuts. Top with whipped cream, if desired.

Mixed Berry Cobbler

MAKES 8 SERVINGS

1 package (16 ounces) frozen mixed berries

½ cup granulated sugar

2 tablespoons quick-cooking tapioca

2 teaspoons grated lemon peel

1½ cups all-purpose flour

½ cup packed light brown sugar

2¼ teaspoons baking powder

¼ teaspoon ground nutmeg

½ cup milk

⅓ cup butter, melted

Vanilla ice cream (optional)

1 Coat inside of **CROCK-POT®** slow cooker with nonstick cooking spray. Stir berries, granulated sugar, tapioca and lemon peel in medium bowl. Remove to **CROCK-POT®** slow cooker.

2 Combine flour, brown sugar, baking powder and nutmeg in medium bowl. Add milk and butter; stir just until blended. Drop spoonfuls of dough on top of berry mixture. Cover; cook on LOW 4 hours.

3 Turn off heat. Uncover; let stand 30 minutes. Serve with ice cream, if desired.

Tip: Cobblers are year-round favorites. Experiment with seasonal fresh fruits, such as pears, plums, peaches, rhubarb, blueberries, raspberries, strawberries, blackberries or gooseberries.

5-Ingredient Kheer

MAKES 6 TO 8 SERVINGS

4	**cups whole milk**
¾	**cup sugar**
1	**cup uncooked white basmati rice, rinsed and drained**
½	**cup golden raisins**

3	**whole green cardamom pods** *or* **¼ teaspoon ground cardamom**
	Strips fresh orange peel (optional)
	Pistachio nuts (optional)

Coat inside of **CROCK-POT**® slow cooker with nonstick cooking spray. Add milk and sugar; stir until sugar is dissolved. Add rice, raisins and cardamom. Cover; cook on HIGH 1 hour. Stir. Cover; cook on HIGH 1½ to 2 hours or until milk has been absorbed. Garnish with orange peel and pistachios.

Cherry Flan

5 eggs

½ cup sugar

½ teaspoon salt

¾ cup all-purpose flour

1 can (12 ounces) evaporated milk

1 teaspoon vanilla

1 bag (16 ounces) frozen pitted dark sweet cherries, thawed

   Whipped cream (optional)

   Fresh cherries (optional)

   Sprigs fresh mint (optional)

1 Coat inside of **CROCK-POT**® slow cooker with nonstick cooking spray. Beat eggs, sugar and salt in large bowl with electric mixer at high speed until thick and pale yellow. Add flour; beat until smooth. Beat in evaporated milk and vanilla.

2 Pour batter into **CROCK-POT**® slow cooker. Place frozen cherries evenly over batter. Cover; cook on LOW 3½ to 4 hours or until flan is set. Serve warm with whipped cream, if desired. Garnish each serving with fresh cherries and mint.

Chili Verde (page 41)

Metric Conversion Chart

VOLUME MEASUREMENTS (dry)

1/8 teaspoon = 0.5 mL
1/4 teaspoon = 1 mL
1/2 teaspoon = 2 mL
3/4 teaspoon = 4 mL
1 teaspoon = 5 mL
1 tablespoon = 15 mL
2 tablespoons = 30 mL
1/4 cup = 60 mL
1/3 cup = 75 mL
1/2 cup = 125 mL
2/3 cup = 150 mL
3/4 cup = 175 mL
1 cup = 250 mL
2 cups = 1 pint = 500 mL
3 cups = 750 mL
4 cups = 1 quart = 1 L

VOLUME MEASUREMENTS (fluid)

1 fluid ounce (2 tablespoons) = 30 mL
4 fluid ounces (1/2 cup) = 125 mL
8 fluid ounces (1 cup) = 250 mL
12 fluid ounces (1½ cups) = 375 mL
16 fluid ounces (2 cups) = 500 mL

WEIGHTS (mass)

1/2 ounce = 15 g
1 ounce = 30 g
3 ounces = 90 g
4 ounces = 120 g
8 ounces = 225 g
10 ounces = 285 g
12 ounces = 360 g
16 ounces = 1 pound = 450 g

DIMENSIONS

1/16 inch = 2 mm
1/8 inch = 3 mm
1/4 inch = 6 mm
1/2 inch = 1.5 cm
3/4 inch = 2 cm
1 inch = 2.5 cm

OVEN TEMPERATURES

250°F = 120°C
275°F = 140°C
300°F = 150°C
325°F = 160°C
350°F = 180°C
375°F = 190°C
400°F = 200°C
425°F = 220°C
450°F = 230°C

BAKING PAN SIZES

Utensil	Size in Inches/Quarts	Metric Volume	Size in Centimeters
Baking or Cake Pan (square or rectangular)	8×8×2	2 L	20×20×5
	9×9×2	2.5 L	23×23×5
	12×8×2	3 L	30×20×5
	13×9×2	3.5 L	33×23×5
Loaf Pan	8×4×3	1.5 L	20×10×7
	9×5×3	2 L	23×13×7
Round Layer Cake Pan	8×1½	1.2 L	20×4
	9×1½	1.5 L	23×4
Pie Plate	8×1¼	750 mL	20×3
	9×1¼	1 L	23×3
Baking Dish or Casserole	1 quart	1 L	—
	1½ quart	1.5 L	—
	2 quart	2 L	—